WHAT THE $ELL AM I DOING WITH MY LIFE?!

Philosophy, Advice and Technique
For a Career in Sales

Allan J. Davenport

In loving memory of my mother, Judith

WHAT THE **$ELL** AM I DOING WITH MY LIFE?!

Introduction

Q&A

Questions**:** Like opinions (and other things), we all have them. From the first day we open our eyes, until the day we close them for good, we ask ourselves and others a seemingly-endless array of questions. If I were to offer you $1 for every question you ever had, wouldn't you have more than enough money to be retired right now? See? Aside from the multitude of questions we ask regarding our personal lives, salespeople of all levels of experience, have many questions whose answers are critical to the success of our daily professional lives. In writing this book, I will do my best to draw upon 20 years of personal experience in sales to answer the following (and hopefully many more) questions for you:

Why would I choose "sales" in my attempt to earn a living in this complicated, ever-changing world? Is "sales" a safe career choice? In fact, is "sales" a career choice at all? What is the risk involved with getting involved in sales? How long does it take to become a viable, highly-skilled, highly-paid salesperson? When I consider the next 20, 30, or 40 plus years of my life, what type of product or service would be best suited for me to represent? How do social and economic factors and changes affect the birth, growth and demise of products, services, companies and industries? How can I monitor those factors so I can at least keep up with, if not, stay ahead of them? What does "the boss" expect of me, likewise, what should I expect of him? Does he even care if I have a life outside his "goldmine"? How much (stuff) do I need to put up with before I realize that it's best just to move on? What can I learn from my peer salespeople? How can we work together, as a team, to achieve better results than we can as individuals? What are some effective "outside the box" ideas I can use in an effort to multiply my company's customers and, more importantly, the dollar amounts on my paychecks? How can I form a real connection to my potential, present and future customers? How can I get more out of them so they can get more out of my product or service? How do I get customers to listen to me? How can I get them to look at me as if I am an actual human being, and not a blood-sucking vampire? How much can I enhance their standards of living and/or qualities of life if they buy this product/service today? How do I conduct more effective, if not "magical", sales presentations? How can I "help" the customer make a decision? How can I make sure I'm not wasting my or the customer's time? More importantly, how do I make sure he's not wasting my time? How do I show my customer that he needs the product or service more than I need to make a sale? Does he really think I get more out of the completion of this deal than he does? How do I handle the potential adversities that may occur before, during and after the point of sale?

What's the difference between someone who "tries" sales and a consistent six-figure earner?

If you are either currently in or considering selling for a living, you will ask yourself every single one of these questions, and more. On top of that, throughout your career, you will be asking questions of others all day long. When you prospect (find, in any way possible) leads and make appointments (sales opportunities), you ask for the opportunity to sell. When on a sales appointment, you ask about the lives and needs of your customers. Upon conclusion of a successful sales demonstration (show-and-tell for grownups), you ask for a commitment to buy. Finally, you ask for some names and numbers of other people to whom you may now ask the same exact questions. Yes, as exciting as it sounds, a life in sales is one consisting of a never-ending cycle of asking the "same old questions".

On the much brighter side, however, many people, including yours truly and others with whom I've peered, have asked "the same old questions" to the tune of earning millions of dollars in income. That's the really funny thing: a repetitious pattern of questions, when pre-planned and handled precisely, makes earning great money laughably easy. The trick of the whole thing, though, is to do the best you can to limit the daily questions to the ones that further your income, as opposed to the ones that bog down your ability to think and perform clearly enough to win. In writing this book, my goal is twofold: To answer that long list of questions you'll undoubtedly have, and help you figure out the questions, and timing thereof, that will help you fulfill your main duties as a professional salesperson: bettering the lifestyles and qualities of life of your customers by committing them to what you sell.

Do you remember Aesop's fable of the tortoise and the hare? Well, if you don't, one of these animals is significantly faster than the other. However, both animals are equipped with legs. Being so, both have the ability to eventually cross the finish line. Today, I consider myself (perhaps some others do as well) to be a highly skilled salesperson. "Today", however, is approximately 20 years removed (and ten thousand-plus sales presentations) from my first day on the job. I, like many others I have worked with and for, began my career, for lack of a better analogy, more like the tortoise than the hare. The fact is, when you are new at anything, it is nearly impossible to be "quick out of the gate". In sales, however, as well as in fables, a strong finish is much more important (and lucrative) than a quick start. Try not to be discouraged at the "starting line" of your career in sales. Everyone experiences the challenges of the "new guy". The winners of the race (and there are more in sales than any other profession by far) push through the awkwardness of being "rookies" so they may eventually reap the financial rewards attained by polished "veterans". This advice may be applied to turtles, rabbits, and you.

Becoming Beethoven?

Should you be able to stay awake while reading this book, you will undoubtedly notice my usage and love of analogies. Here is one involving actual human beings: There have been millions of pianos made for tens of millions of people upon which to learn. Yet, there was only one Beethoven. Unlike such a prodigy, most great pianists actually had to learn to play piano. They didn't just sit down, like Beethoven, and start playing symphonies. For non-prodigal pianists, the difference between "chopsticks" and "Chopin" is each individual's implementation of his teachings.

While there are many highly skilled, highly successful and highly paid salespeople, there are no "Beethovens" among them. Nobody I've ever met started off with considerably more sales ability than anybody else. Certainly, I've met some people whose outgoing personalities seemed pre-disposed to success, yet, everything about the act of selling must be learned and properly applied. The application and the accompanying level of success with it are not a result of an individual's "ear" for music. It is all up to the individual himself. Everyone I've known, including myself, has had "first days" and all of the struggles, if you will, that accompany them. From my own experience, it took about six months "selling" (for lack of a better term) before I became somewhat confident in securing my own buying commitments (some call it "closing deals"). However, after months of sweaty armpits and numerous heart palpitations, selling got easier and I got better. Once I "got it", many of the things I've learned since then just made it easier and easier. Soon enough, I was not only securing my own buying commitments, but I was also securing them for my peers and managers. I actually enjoyed "taking over" other people's sales presentations much more than completing my own. Even though most of my sales life has been spent dealing with my own customers, I've always enjoyed helping others in sales to better deal with their customers.

Now, after 20 years, and thousands of sales and "takeovers", it gives me a renewed excitement to be able to pass on what I've learned from hundreds of other sales-producers, some of whom I consider icons, to (hopefully) millions of other salespeople, regardless of their tenures or achieved levels of success. On that note, please allow me to both acknowledge and thank the greatest sales influences with whom I have been truly blessed to be associated: From Bally Total Fitness; Mike LaManna, Robb Giorgi, Carmine DiPietro, Michael Espinosa, and the great Jerry Espinosa Auto sales; James Dollinger, Kenneth Moore, and Mel Hampton Timeshare sales; Willard Durant Directbuy; Don Felix, Bart Fesperman, and Scott Powell AvMed; Dana Ottaviano. Without the significant influences of these people, you, my dear reader, would be reading something else. As far as I'm concerned, I owe them my life. If you are reading this now, I thank you with everything I (think I) know. During the last 2 years of brain-frying writing and rewriting, as the aforementioned would have required, I have done the very best job I can to deliver solid and useful philosophy, advice and technique to you. I sincerely hope you get at least one, if not very many, good idea that can make your sales life easier, more fun and way, way, (way) more lucrative.

Although today I wouldn't consider any job that wasn't sales- related, I freely admit to having spent nearly my entire first year questioning whether or not "sales" was the proper career choice for me. Instead of unproductive thinking like that, take my advice and just get serious about selling. Do the things that I, and other experienced salespeople and managers, show you to do, in the way that they should be done. Wholeheartedly believe that if you stick it out, things (and you) will get better. I've seen too many good people (with a ton of potential) give up much too easily. Many of them were right on the edge of breaking through the initial barriers, with which we all struggle, on our way to becoming successful salespeople. I am writing this because, on the contrary, I want you to experience all the things that both I and many others truly love about sales and the act of selling: the internal and financial rewards associated with bettering the lives of others. Life is tough. However, wouldn't you agree that it would be a little easier to navigate through its various travails with a six-figure income?

Who's looking out for your career?

When you think about the various agendas with which the people in your life have, let me be one who is up front with his. After all, when we seek advice in answering the many questions that we have, isn't it important that we fully understand the agenda of the person from which the advice is being sought? When you consider the people in your life, with respect to your career, whose agenda most resembles yours? "The boss" wants (demands) professional life to be your entire life. Your significant other wants (demands) that your personal life take precedence your work life. The aforementioned influences will be in constant conflict with each other for the rest of your professional and personal lives. As aggravating as that may sound, you might as well get used to it now. Your friends certainly want you to be happy, but they are generally completely unaffected by your financial success or lack thereof. (Unless, of course, they are the type of "friends" who expect you to pay the bar tab) Your fellow salesperson may be friendly with you, but he also competes against you for adulation and/or advancement in the workplace. When you choose to take sales career advice from any of these people, as much as they may care about you, they all have biases that support their own agendas. In the end, any decisions you make will affect all of those people, but, most of all, you.

I, too, am not without agenda. My agenda, however, is to sell books (millions upon millions if possible). The only way for me to attain the goal of my agenda is to make you a better (and much more highly paid) salesperson. The only reason that I should have the opportunity to enter your life is to help enhance it monetarily. To accomplish this, I will do my best to help you assimilate 20 years of sales education and experience into your daily sales life within a few hours. (Sounds simple, doesn't it?)

I am not some sort of motivational sales "guru" who is here to bore you to death with 300 pages of "how I made my first 100 million". Aside from the fact that I have earned far less than 100 million dollars, with respect to the value of your precious time, I promise to bore you to death while using less than half the ink! My (weak) sense of humor aside, I have, over time, developed a set of skills that have enabled me (and soon you) to earn six figures in annual commission during the first year of any sales job, regardless of the strength of the economy. In fact, my best years were the US economy's worst. How many salespeople (or anyone) do you know that consider 2007 and 2008 (the worst economic time since the Great Depression of 1929) their best financial years? It is, with respect to my "no excuses" attitude about earning great money regardless of the state of the economy, that I feel my knowledge and advice may be of use to others who have also chosen sales as their career. Hopefully, upon reading this, you will agree.

Although I am not writing a book that is the length of "War and Peace" I do plan to cover a vast number of topics. As I cover these topics, please keep in mind that opinions expressed are solely based on my perception of what I've learned and experienced throughout 20 years of selling. Please feel free to agree or disagree with each one of them. Agreement would be great since the information is useful and, thus, will be helpful. Disagreement, although it will certainly lead you to failure and empty pockets, is fine as well. I am, of course, kidding about the latter. You and I are different people, under different circumstances, with different priorities. Being so, I would expect you to make different choices in how you deal with your personal circumstances. The way I see it, whether you agree or disagree with certain points, my overall goal is to give you unbiased opinions, from salesperson to salesperson, and then allow all the time you need to make your own decisions. In the end, if anything I've written causes you to think and/or grow as a professional salesperson, we both win. It is, when you really think about it, disagreement with opinions and status quo that prompted all of the really good changes that we've seen over time in this country. In fact, if my memory serves correct, it was disagreement with the ways of our founding father's original countries that led to the very formation of this one. If I am able to complete the goal of my agenda and help you become a better salesperson, all I ask is that you help me further my agenda by referring "What the $ell Am I Doing with My Life?!" as a quality resource to your peer salesperson. Fair enough? If I can help you, and you can help someone else, and he can help someone else, won't we all be better off?

How can I help you help me help you?

Out of all of the aspects of selling (many of which we will discuss), most people I've worked with and for know me best for my ability to "close" deals or, as I term it, "securing the commitment to buy." From the day I learned to secure my first buying commitment, I've prided myself in the ability to sell a high percentage of my sales opportunities. As my former employers would gladly attest, I was never crazy about making tons of appointments. So, early on, I stressed the quality of my demonstration and commitment-securing processes over making a large quantity of phone calls. To me, more productivity while selling appointments, meant less time on the phone (begrudgingly) making appointments. In short, better "face to face" meant less "face to phone". What would you rather make: appointments or money? I thought so.

Obviously an appointment must be made with someone, by someone, in order for there to be a sales opportunity. This book, however, is not about making appointments. It is about everything that happens after the point of initial customer contact. It is about the process that transforms an idea in someone's head into dollars in someone else's pocket. The company for whom you work has a lead-generating and appointing process in which you will, most assuredly, be involved. There is also (most likely) a thoroughly developed marketing plan for you to follow in an effort to make sales "their way", which, by the way, is just fine with me. I am not writing this book to teach your company how to do its job. I'm just trying to help you do yours better.

(Anti) Social media

   At the time of writing, I am 41 years of age. For the first half of my life, people didn't use computers for work. I used them to play video games, albeit less harmful ones than people play today. Throughout the next half, however, almost overnight, everyone began using them for everything. Today, babies are born with power cords, replacing the umbilical cords of past generations. My generation grew up in between the "face to face" generations of the past and the "face to screen" generations of the present and future. It is my belief that people in my age group can offer a unique perspective on life both with and prior to the internet. We are the last generation that grew up having to talk to each other sans computer screen. It is, with that in mind, that one of my intentions with this book is to help build a bridge between the widening social gap that the technology of the present has enabled us to (ever so lazily) create by focusing my writing on the interpersonal aspects of selling, which has made so many salespeople successful in the past. Effective selling will be a thing of the past if we completely lose sight of the interpersonal aspect of it.

Don't get me wrong: I'm not against the socially-connective aspect of the internet, just the anti-social results of our reliance upon it. When we choose to make proper use of them, computers can serve a salesperson's purpose by spreading benefit to others in ways he obviously can't do as an individual person. What I cannot stand, however, is how some people use them to shield themselves from the consequences of cowardly bashing friends and colleagues through the many forms of "social" media. If you are interested a computer barely-literate's advice, a simple rule of thumb (all puns intended) with regards to the use of social media would this: Would you ever actually say whatever it is you are about to "enter" directly to a person's face? If so, be a real "grown-up" and do just that. If not, save the impending embarrassment you are likely to endure due to the decision to "shoot" before you think. Take time to consider the consequences before you "tweet" because, once it's out in cyberspace, you can't take it back. Don't help the technology at your fingertips sabotage your career and/or ruin your life the way it already has some professional athletes, politicians and others. It remains to be seen if we, as human beings, are responsible enough or even capable of properly dealing with our current and future technological capabilities. The very scary thing is that it is really up to us. If you promise to be careful with technology, I will gladly return the favor by promising to sound less like my dad.

Definitely!

There will be many times (should you elect to continue reading) throughout this book that I reference the "*Webster's Dictionary*". As tedious as that may sound, as a sales professional, it is my opinion that it is always best to speak in definite terms. As we have all experienced, when we leave points we are attempting to make solely up to the imagination of others, they have a great chance of being horribly and disastrously misinterpreted.

This book is about selling. Selling, as defined by *Webster's*, is to promote the sale and purchase of a product or service. While promoting the sale of your chosen product or service you have two goals: securing the commitment to buy and growing and furthering your own "business within the business." Every second (minus meals, which are vital to every productive brain) of your business day must revolve around achieving those goals.

According to *Webster's*, securing is the act of making certain, a commitment is a promise to do something, and buying is defined as the act of obtaining by paying with money. Therefore, securing the commitment to buy can be defined as the result of a salesperson making certain that a customer promises to obtain a product or service by handing said salesperson his money.

The "business within the business" is the sum-total of all of the contributing factors that make the securing of commitments to buy possible for all salespeople throughout their careers. It is a combination all of the skills they learn and refine, the people they present, the ones who choose to become their customers, their sales environment (workplace, boss, coworkers, etc.) and how they employ all of them for their own greater good. (A mega-prosperous career based on doing right by others.)

Those brave souls, for whom the task is to secure commitments to buy, will be referred to as "salespeople" (or individually as salesperson). Over the last 20 years or so, a potentially earth-imploding beast known as "political correctness" (an oxymoron if there ever was one) has tried to rename salespeople "consultants". To me, that is nothing but a superficial tool that companies use to make customers think their salespeople care about them. Care is an unspoken "must-have" for any successful salesperson. To me, consultants listen to their clients, and then make recommendations for change. A salesperson does both exactly that and solidly ensure that the recommended change take place. A consultant will, often times, allow his client to get less out of life because he does not want to risk agitating him. On the other hand, a salesperson knows that, sometimes, agitation is just part of the job. In short, while consultants may suggest change, salespeople make change happen.

As far as gender is concerned, with regard to both salespeople and customers, everyone in this book will be referred to as "he" or "him". Although there are many female salespeople that ridiculously outperform their male counterparts, physically typing "him/her" or "he/she" is just too much work for me. As you can tell from the laziness, I am male.

Let's go "Krazy"!

My overall view of the goal in selling reminds me of an interesting television commercial I saw many thousands of times as a child. The product was a super-adhesive named Krazy Glue. During this commercial, a construction worker applies Krazy Glue to the top of his helmet and attaches it to the bottom of a steel girder. Then, he literally (or as literal as television commercials get) risks his life by hanging off the girder to demonstrate the power of his purchase. The bond created by the adhesive was so strong that he was willing to go far outside his comfort zone (and general safety, not to mention common sense) in an effort to promote its usefulness. The main goal in sales is to create a bond between a customer and a product or service that rivals the aforementioned strength. After all, not all glues bind with the strength of Krazy Glue, do they? The stronger the bond you create, the better your chance will be to secure the customer's commitment to the sale. The more you are willing to repeat the process with the utmost precision, the more likely you are to add many thousands of new (paying) customers. So, just exactly do you create that bond?

You should create the bond by establishing and strengthening the connections between you and selling in general, the right product or service, the optimal work environment, and the relationships you establish with the customer and him to the product or service. The strength of these connections will directly affect the overall strength of the bond. Let us now examine each connection in the order in which they appear in every salesperson's life.

I.   Why the Sell?!: Your connection to Sales

Bail, bail, bail, your boat…

When my brother and I were young (at a time in history when one could press the number on a phone instead of having to wait an hour for the "O" to get back in position) a bailout was the action we took when our leaky 12 foot skiff took on too much water. In an attempt to stay afloat, one of us (likely him, as he is younger) would take an old "Fluff" (a delicious spread that compliments any peanut butter and jelly sandwich) container and bailout our sinking skiff. Once we returned to shore (all of 200 feet away) we would "repair" the bottom of the aluminum boat by filling the hole with warm tar. The tar, as pliable as "silly putty", was quite useful for our filling and sealing purposes. Unfortunately, due to the increasing pressure on the tar-filled cracks, the skiff would eventually leak once again. As a result, time and time again, he and I would bailout and re-tar our sinking boat. Being children, we did not have the means to buy another boat every time we used it in water that was too shallow which, of course, led to the scraping of the bottom, resulting in the leakage. That's ok, though. As a kid, you'll put a band-aid on little (although continuous) problems because you lack the knowledge and/or capital to fix the real problem every time you "set sail" (all of 200 feet) into the vast Atlantic Ocean.

The sun has risen all fallen 365 and one quarter days more than 30 full times since that day. I can now command my cell phone to find the voice and face of anyone in the world, no matter where he or I happen to physically be located at the time. Yes, a lot has changed in this world in those 30 years. The concept of the bailout, however, apparently hasn't changed at all. I still spend a great deal of my time and money bailing out sinking ships. These ships, though, have taken on much different forms. Now, with the "help" of the government, instead of my 12 foot skiff, I'm bailing out "Titanic" auto manufacturers, banks, Wall Street and countless other industries of which I am totally unaware. With our "Fluff" buckets in hand, you and I (along with all future generations to come) are going to be bailing out sinking ships like the aforementioned and others for the rest of our lives. Sounds awesome, doesn't it? Whether we like it or not, we will be paying the price for their bad decisions, lack of profitability and gross misdirection (I'm being nice). We have to live "closer to the vest" and "tighten our belts" because these companies and many others refused to do the same even after it was too late. Sadly, although we will never be in control of someone else's level of productivity or profitability, someone will always find a way for us to pay for it. In this life, you'll be bailing everyone else out anyway. Why not add yourself to the list? Bail yourself out with a sale a day, and keep the sharks away.

Compete to win

You, me and many reading this, were competitive (academically and/or athletically) from the day we started crawling from room to room. I for one, wish to remain competitive until my only physical activity becomes, once again, crawling from room to room. Whether we compete with someone else or ourselves, every challenge elicits an adrenaline rush that makes us feel alive. There is an exhilaration we feel when we put ourselves "out there" and give it our best possible effort to win.

As kids, we all compete with our brothers, sisters, and other kids in the neighborhood. Growing up, many of us were on some type of competitive team or teams. Some of the greatest times of our lives are had when we are trying our best to help the team win. From a very young age, we learn to enjoy being vital to the success of something. Then there comes the day when our competitive options begin to narrow. For instance, what percentage of high school football players continue on to college and then turn professional? Try a lottery ticket: it causes less bruising!

Where can you find a challenge after you've stopped competing for letters on the report card or the jacket? The thrill of competition is making something positive happen when all external factors (opponents) are working as hard as they can against your success. It is that feeling that surges through you when you've overcome all the adversity that's been thrust upon you. If you are truly competitive, you are exhaustedly elated when victorious and absolutely miserable when you lose. As adults, the average job with average pay almost requires you to abandon your competitive history and "toe the line" while performing boring tasks that never change. No offense, but what's the thrill in being stuck in an unchallenging rut, earning 600 bucks per week today, tomorrow, and forever? Should a person who performs extremely high-quality work "earn" the exact same paycheck as the guy who "sleepwalks" through his shift? Why would anyone choose to work hard if the quality of their work didn't translate to anything concrete, such as lots of cash? Am I knocking the guy who wants a steady job, steady pay and set hours? Not at all. There is something to be said about consistency. However, as we go forward from today, do "steady jobs" even exist anymore? Instead, I would rather compete to win the prize (again, lots of cash). To find worthy competition in sales, look no further than other similar companies, salespeople, and yourself. Every new day presents the challenge of winning a new game. At the start of the day, the score is 0-0 in the game of "you versus bankruptcy". At the end of the day, your efforts will determine the loser and winner of the game. Selling is just like playing back yard football: winners celebrate, losers walk.

No risk, all reward: Is that how the saying goes?

One of the most appealing aspects of "Why the Sell?!" is the risk/reward factor for the salesperson. When you really think about it, a salesperson's job is to make a profit on someone else's risk. Although we pay no business expenses, we earn commission from the sale of its product or service. There is no risk on the salesperson's behalf whatsoever. The product, training, marketing approach and customers are all there at no risk to you. The reward, of course, comes in the form of a (hopefully) healthy commission.

The only possible risk is associated with the development of your personal sales ability. Personally, I have never looked at sales ability as a risk because, with willingness, it is actually quite easy to gain. Believe me: the guy sitting at the desk, office, or cubicle next to you is not a retired rocket scientist! There are many things on this earth more difficult to master than selling skills. All you really need to do is learn and practice the few simple methods that sell your product or service to others and apply them consistently throughout your daily sales life. Congratulations! In sales, you have found a "no risk/all reward" career in a "no risk/no reward" world.

You need to come to grips with it quickly: a college education alone is not going to earn you a cozy job, office, and retirement. Maybe it did for my dad and his friends (back when the TV show "Mad Men" was real life).You and I (and those who come after us) don't have 40 hour work weeks. We aren't guaranteed to retire at age 65. The hands of time aren't magically going to turn back to the "good old days" no matter who we bail out. Be productive and bail yourself out through selling or sink along with the other leaky ships. I don't know for sure, yet I suspect life is best enjoyed above sea level, far above the ocean floor. (Unless, of course, you are scuba diving on vacation)

I am 41 years old and I first heard the "new" term bailout used a couple years ago. My bet (and I don't, of course, because gambling is illegal in most states) is that I will hear that term used repeatedly until I die. Personally, (I hope I can speak for you as well) I don't want to spend my (all too limited) time on earth worrying about money. When I think about "Why the Sell?!" that's more than enough to convince me. Money, which you will earn every time you make a sale, doesn't cure all of your problems, but it will cure the financial ones. As you do, little by little, you will fill the "Fluff bucket" with money and, ultimately, keep your head well above the ever-rising level of water enveloping the rest of the world.

In view of the fact that different types of products and services will come and go, selling was here long before us and will endure long after we pass. The surety of sales lasting the test of time is right up there with death and taxes. (In a good way, though) Because this is a fact, this world will always need highly skilled salespeople. Whether or not 10+ % of our population sits unemployed, great salespeople are not among that group. They are selling something, somewhere, to someone in all economies; good, bad and ugly. Sometimes they make a lot of money; sometimes they don't. They are, however, for the most part, in complete control over the dollar amounts in their paychecks. In sales, as my dad might say, producers get paid, while parasites look for bailouts. Before you choose "sales" as a career, you must first choose whether to live as a parasite or a producer. I guarantee you will enjoy one life a lot more than the other!

In closing, let me say that bailouts have done a heck of a job decimating the capitalist society I always dreamed of entering as a kid. As an adult, frankly, I am sick of it! I'm sick of sitting idly by, on the sidelines, watching our beloved country sink farther below sea level every second. Are you sick enough of it, as well, to use your competitive juices in a no risk/all reward career to rise above it? For all of our sakes, I certainly hope so!

II. What the Sell?!: Your Connection to a Product or Service

Express your (REAL) self

The first, and most important connection to make, is the one that exists between you and the product or service you choose to represent. Why should this be considered the first connection? You need to be completely connected to, as if one-with, whatever it is you sell if you are ever going to convince someone else to buy and use it. Why would someone else buy it if you didn't use it? For instance, was the guy who sold you the health club membership 40 pounds overweight? Is the guy who sold you the timeshare someone who has never been on vacation? Did you see the guy who sold you your last Toyota at the grocery store with his Ford Mustang?

Contradictions between what we sell and how we live are the type of inconsistencies that can doom a potentially successful career in sales. When inconsistencies exist, customers think we are lying. And, we should all know by now, lying is no way to establish credibility. The biggest reason your job is so difficult today is because of the failure of your predecessors in sales to be consistent and credible. That is why there is a giant obstacle in front of you, in the form of a general lack of trust, every time you attempt to deal with a new customer. Do yourself a huge favor: be part of the solution, not part of the problem.

Put your money where your mouth is. Don't ever push an investment on someone else that you wouldn't first make yourself. What do you think would make you a more effective representative of a certain product or service: simply knowing something about it, or actually owning and using it? I am not suggesting that you go out and spend money that you don't have to invest in the product that you sell today, but you will not form a solid connection until you do. If you do not fully connect with the product or service, you have little or no chance of selling it over the long haul of your sales life. If you don't love your product the way an investing consumer should, you are not likely to stick with it when the times are less fruitful. Like any marriage, this connection should be solid in times of health as in times of sickness, right? Always keep in mind that every product or service must be sold to someone by someone. Fortunately for you, the category of "everything" makes it very possible for you to find at least something to which you can create a solid, lasting bond.

Who knows?

Professionally, not many things are more embarrassing to a salesperson than the discovery that his potential customer knows more about the product or service he represents than he does. I'm quite sure of that, as I've found myself in the same position many times in the past. The customer is in front of you today because he is seeking professional advice. Today's customer will only trust an expert when considering potential uses for his hard-earned "disposable" income. Money aside, don't you think it makes sense to really know what you're talking about before you open our mouth? (Unless, of course, you love the taste of an inserted foot)

A salesperson's constant willingness gain product knowledge is the first step in establishing his short and long term value to customers, his company, and himself. That is not to say that the auto salesperson needs to be as adept at vehicle diagnostics as the dealership's mechanics, but he should never have a problem opening up the hood of a car. Laugh all you want, but I've resembled that remark in the past. The corresponding embarrassment I suffered due to the ineptitude was, to say the least, not fun. Would it really kill you to learn five or six important components of the vehicle you sell? If it would kill you, please risk your life selling something else. Find the product or service for which you have enough passion to be both a consistent student and highly capable teacher.

Your product and customer have changed over time. As is the trend, they will continue to change. Don't you feel that it would be best if your knowledge were to stay ahead of those changes? How would you compare your level of product knowledge to that of the best salesperson in your field? The quick answer to that question can be seen by looking directly at each other's paychecks. Wouldn't you want yours to look more like his? Me too!

Your best sources of product information are contained within the materials at your place of business. My advice to you: peruse the materials that further educate you about the product or service you represent at least 30 minutes everyday. This will "wake up" your mind and provide you the enthusiasm to share your knowledge with others as you help them increase their standard of living and/or quality of life.

It is one thing to know a lot about a product. An individual's ability to transfer said product from the store shelf to the customer's home is an entirely separate issue. Learning the skills it takes to achieve this is as important as the product knowledge itself. These are the skills that separate those who fix cars from those who sell cars. The never ending honing and refining of these skills is what separates the average-earning salesperson from that of the six-figure professional salesperson.

As previously discussed, selling is competitive. Myself, and many people I know have analogized it with athletic competition. For instance, what are three things that can be said about Michael Jordan, Tiger Woods and Tom Brady? Number one, they are/were among the very best ever at their chosen professions. Secondly, they are all (beyond) multi-millionaires. Most importantly, they all have the reputation (among other things) of putting in significantly more quality practice time than that of their opponents. To these men, the difference between winning and losing is all about the quality of the preparation. Do you disagree? Like these legendary athletes, salespeople must also be legendary on the "practice field". Of course, for us practice doesn't (officially) involve working on jump-shots. The sales professional "practices" through role playing selling scenarios with his peers. By working together, the role "players" become better equipped to deal with the hurdles that arise while making their living trying to improve the lives of others.

Here, from my experience, are your best sources of sales training information: your business, for one, should have its own version of sales training technique pertaining to the product or service it represents. This technique will coincide with the specific marketing plan of the business. It is "their way" to sell. Outside of the specific business, today there are also books like this one and others that contain every technique and point of view on the topic of selling. I am among many who, wholeheartedly, believe that a professional invests his time and (in the case of this book) money to enhance his sales skills. A percentage of our personal incomes should always go toward the bettering of ourselves and what we hope to accomplish on a professional level. Hopefully that percentage somewhat rivals the amount you spend at the bar destroying those precious brain cells upon which you, most vitally, rely.

Thirdly, and perhaps most useful in your quest to gain sales knowledge, is your fellow salesperson. I owe the greatest debt of gratitude to those few caring salespeople who chose to become my mentors. Previously, you read the names of the people I consider as important to my professional development as my internal organs are to my very existence. No matter what business you are in, there is somebody there who has, does and will experience a tremendous amount of success at what he sells. He also knows that he owes a lot of the success he's attained to those whom he befriended, as they taught and guided him when he was "the new guy". As the evolution of sales and selling goes, he should feel the obligation to mentor someone else as well, as do I.

Do yourself the biggest favor of your entire life by endearing yourself, in any way possible, (up to, and surpassing, your purchase of his daily coffee) to this person. Become the lucky one upon whom he will choose to impart his valuable time and skills. Do everything he says and everything he does. Don't argue with him until you are more adept at selling than he is. At that point, only argue constructively, for the betterment of both of your careers. If you can do that, then you may someday reach or surpass his level of success. Staying true to the code, you will then be obligated to further the evolution of sales by mentoring another "rookie" like yourself. (If you are an established veteran, please disregard the last three words of the previous sentence. Thank you.) By writing this book, I am trying to fulfill the same obligation to my mentors.

By the way, you will not find your mentor huddled together in a group of salespeople, whining about the terrible state of the economy, quality of the leads and/or the lack of traffic being generated by the business. Your mentor is not waiting for something to happen; he is the one who is pushing the process of making it happen. After all, making it happen makes him money. Fortunately, by reading this right now, you are starting to make it happen too.

Social and economic impacts

"What the Sell?!" is the product or service that connects your past, present and future. In combination with your personal interests, "What the Sell?!" becomes your natural professional life. How did the past affect the person you presently are? How do you see yourself in the future? "What the Sell?!" is the result of an agreement between who you are, who you wish to be, and the product or service that agrees most with that progression. The more natural your connection to it, the more naturally willing you will be to connect others to it. Where the (heck) does someone find something that fits that description on this planet? Everywhere!

How is this possible? It is because "What the Sell?!" is not only an expression of you, (the person you are and aspire to be) but also the same type of expression of your potential customers (everyone else in the world). Considering the fact that there are more than 7 billion people on this planet, one needn't be a geneticist to realize that you share similarities to at least a million of them (give or take). Our similarities to each other have the tendency to group us together. They serve as proof that the human being is, in fact, a "social animal". Even though most of us would gladly do without our fellow man (or woman), we know that we really need them in our lives. Other people perform a variety of functions that lend to the overall ease of our existence. Other people are a necessity to us. Just look around: Who made the things you own, the clothes you wear, or even the food you eat? I would bet (with gambling still illegal) that it was someone else who did all that for you and others.

What do all of those people that provide those products and services have in common with each other? Much like you, they get paid to produce. Why is it so important for everybody out there to get paid? The human being is not just a social animal, but an economic one as well. This country was actually founded a couple hundred years ago by people who came from other countries of a few thousand years of age because of its economic potential. Throughout its short history, this country's ability to produce agriculture, precious metals and other resources are both impressive and well documented. How much gold, iron ore, oil, etc., have we already extracted from it? How many (legal) crops have we grown?

Needless to say, this country has undergone both tremendous growth and change since the pilgrims first landed. For "What the Sell?!" purposes, I will give examples of how both social and economic changes, over the last 40 years of my life, have evolved some of today's businesses. I firmly believe that, by paying close attention to past and present social and economic issues, we become more equipped to predict the future of any sales business. Here are some examples from my personal sales life:

Fitness for dummies?

My sales first job was in health club membership sales. Having grown up a competitive skier and track athlete, I was what some might call a "fitness junkie." (This is an oxymoron, as I both lifted weights and ate tons of junk food.) Proper nutrition aside, as an expert in physical fitness, making money by selling the idea of better shape and health to other people was very appealing to me. The real "What the Sell?!" quality to me was that the health club was a place to which I would naturally gravitate when I wasn't working. The fact that I went there for fun helped make my work life more fun. Do you automatically gravitate to the product or service you represent even when you're not getting paid? If you do, in my opinion, you are headed in the right direction. During my 20's, the health club provided, in the form of a workplace, an environment that reflected both who I was at the time and whom I wished to remain in the future. It also provided the environment in which I could serve the fitness needs of thousands of other people.

That was, however, in the early 1990's. Health and fitness was the "in" thing at the time. By that time, social change had not only made a career in health and fitness membership sales possible, but also extremely profitable. Just a few years before, when I was a bit younger, there weren't very many health clubs. In the early 1970's, toned muscles were only useful to, as explained to me by my beloved, chain-smoking grandma, "dummies who have to make money with their backs, not their brains". Back then, social perception equated large muscles to small intellects. From the same perspective, cigarette smoking was not only highly accepted, but glamorous. At the same time "dummies" across America were exercising in the few gyms they could find, "smart" people were smoking cigarettes in airplanes, hospital rooms, restaurants, and right into the faces (and lungs) of their loved ones.

A lot had changed in the short amount of time between my conversation with Grandma and my first day on the job. The deteriorating health of the cigarette-smoking populace led to numerous studies that linked smoking directly to cancer (ie: death). It was, at that time, that many people began to figure out that developing lean muscle led to a much better quality of life than the muscle wasting that was associated with not exercising regularly and smoking cigarettes. As a result, the population of the United States rapidly got "dumber". Numerous health clubs and bans on smoking (ie: airplanes, hospitals, restaurants, etc.) started popping up all over the place. Today, the last generation to glorify the cigarette is dying off. Smokers are the modern version of biblical lepers: they are shunned and separated from their healthier peers. Beginning now, an aggressive sales person can make a great living serving the needs and desires of "dummies" who wish to spend their lives improving their cardiovascular and muscular health.

If you need any further evidence of how social change spawns economic opportunity, just look at the birth and growth of the "stop smoking" business. How many millions (if not billions) of dollars per year are generated just to get people to stop smoking? Due to the social change of the last generation on the topics of smoking and exercising, future generations will be born innately knowing that smoking is dumb and exercising is smart. The choice will be (as it always was) theirs to make: smart or dumb? Hopefully, they will choose the right one.

How will the future of the health and fitness industry affect our country's future economic situation? For one, fitter employees miss less time at work due to sick days and other onset health issues of the unfit. This fact, coupled with an increased focus from leading a healthy lifestyle, increase an employee's overall productivity. They tend to waste less physician time and insurance/prescription money. In other words, fit employees cost their employers less than unfit employees. Add to that, the cost of researching and curing exercise-preventable diseases such as heart disease and diabetes, etc., and you, my friend, have a heck of a lot of economic reason for people to live a heck of a lot healthier. On top of that, the ten minutes it takes the average employee to get back and forth to the company's designated smoking area every hour, costs businesses about one hour per day (one month per year) in productive work. I'm just saying…

Strength in auto sales numbers

Let us now take a look at how economic change has affected auto industry sales in the last 40 years. Most people, whether they live by themselves or with their families, have the need for individual transportation. As my favorite sales manager, Ken Moore, said to me, "this is America. And in America everybody does two things: everybody eats and everybody drives". He said this on oft occasion along with the obligatory "unless you live in New York City, and this ain't New York City". Although he was referring to "The City's" mass-transit system, Ken was right. We were in Flint, Michigan. If you haven't had the "pleasure" of visiting Flint, please allow me to save you the trip: it ain't New York City! Having always been eager to make as many sales as I possibly could, prospecting "everybody" was quite an intoxicating attraction. "Everybody", however, doesn't all purchase the exact same type/manufacturer of vehicle.

How do people narrow down their choices of all the different types of vehicles there are? Here's how I looked at it: Although cars and trucks have been around for over 100 years, please allow me to refer back to the 1970's. The first words I remember hearing over and again (aside from "no, you can't have another cookie") were "gas" and "crisis". Rising inflation, OPEC and our country's growing reliance on the consumption of oil led to the beginning of a 40 year (and counting) skyrocketing price of gas. As a result, the average American family was (figuratively) scared to death of how much it would cost to drive from point A to point B. Sound familiar? The consumer's lack of desire to spend his work life filling his tank led to the need for a more fuel-efficient engine. Technology would be necessary to help the average driver get more mileage for his money. That was the thinking behind the birth of the economy car.

Unknown foreign auto manufacturers (ie: Toyota, Honda and other current giants) were beginning to infiltrate the US auto market with smaller, more economic vehicles. Showcasing their superior fuel efficiency, these manufacturers were quickly replacing the two ton, gas-guzzling deathtraps driven by our parents with vehicles that fit our changing economic needs. From a social standpoint, however, the country that prompted the United States' involvement in World War II couldn't possibly succeed in selling anything on our soil, could they? In other words, John Belushi, it wasn't the Germans who bombed Pearl Harbor. Being that Asian and American relations were not as "rosy" as they are today, most every car on the block was made by one of the three big US auto manufacturers.

Almost suddenly, against the patriotic feelings of most American people, the US auto manufacturer was challenged by foreign competitors that had been accepted by its own customer base. From that point on, the once-foreign auto makers continued to make more economic vehicles, gain market share and spend more time, effort, and money than the US manufacturer on important things such as research and design. If that weren't enough, the newer automakers learned how to avoid extra costs (of many different types) that our US based and employed manufacturers could not. As a result, they offered the average consumer a better looking, more efficient, and lower priced vehicle than the "big three". At the same time, the U.S. automakers were "combating" Japanese automakers with various slogans that implored the U.S. consumer to "buy American."

Without knowing all of the actual history between then (1975) and today, how do you think the two different groups of auto manufacturers ended up? Over the last ten years, the financial woes, near doom, and subsequent taxpayer-subsidized government bailout of the US automaker have been well documented. So, too, is the case of the simultaneous rise of newer manufacturers like Hyundai. In Hyundai's case, on top of following the superior auto design trends of the other foreign automakers, they offered a ten year/100,000 mile warranty. Due to the fact that they had effectively eliminated the post-purchase repair costs that frustrate all auto owners, Hyundai has been able to consistently gain market share while the US manufacturer fends off extinction. It would make sense, considering how the price of cars has escalated since the 1970's, (you could get some of them for less than $1,000) that if you were able to keep repair costs to zero, there might be more money left over to purchase a new car quicker. If your goal is to sell cars for at least the next 20 years, look for the ones that lead in economy, safety and warranty. When those qualities are present, the price of the vehicle won't matter.

Share time, make money!

Now let's examine how social and economic change affected the growth of the vacation timeshare industry. I don't know just when, exactly, the first time a family went away to vacation together, but I do know that I enjoyed many great family vacations. My parents, like many others, wanted their children to have more when they grew up than they did. In my family (among other things), that meant taking one or two nice vacations per year.

It may sound "Flintstone" age, but when I was younger (for the most part), dads went to work and moms maintained the home. The title "man of the house" actually meant something back then. Today, the "man" of my house is the largest cat. By the time I was a teenager, the cost of living had risen so much (as it always has and will), dads and moms were both working somewhere, between part and full time. Soon after, both parents were working two to three jobs to try to make ends meet.

However, as work opportunity was increasing, the family connection was deteriorating. The growing demands on everyone's time transformed time spent with the family, that used to be taken for granted, into a very precious commodity. Our lack of time has created a growing need for quality time. In order to make that time to be extra-special, many families would opt to take the family away on vacation.

Now, of course, in order to go on vacation for a week, a family needs a place to stay. Until the 1970's, aside from becoming buddies with the snobby neighbor who owned a second home, the options were to either buy a home solely for the purpose of vacation or to "throw money away" by renting a hotel room. I don't care what decade it is; if families can barely afford the mortgage payments (on top of all the other bills) on their primary homes, how could they even consider carrying two mortgages at once?

With vast numbers of families booking vacations the only way they could afford them, hoteliers started running up the rates. Due to a little-known term that I affectionately call "supply and demand", a hotel room that could be booked for $50 per night in 1980 is likely ten times more expensive today. Do people earn significantly more money today than they did in the mid 1980's? No they don't. So how does a family expect to pay $400 per day (around $3,000 per week) for one tiny room in which to stuff the entire family? What about the extra $200-$300 per day ($1,500 per week) to feed the family at tourist- gauging restaurants? The average family can't pop $5,000-

$6,000 per year (plus travel expenses) to spend quality time (stuffed in one room) together. The bitter reality is that a large majority of them are either forced to stay home during vacation time or to "make friends" with their snobby neighbors who own vacation homes.

In order to keep selling units at resorts, smart developers started selling units of time (sort of like when a pizza maker bakes a whole pie and then sells individual slices). After all, developers only care about building and selling. They couldn't care less whom it was using the units. Now, by sharing the expenses, families could own and use the exact amount of time they needed for their families. Aside from not having to "pop" two to three hundred thousand dollars for a second home, a family could enjoy all the comforts of one without having to worry about finding a way to maintain it the whole year round. Instead, they could now invest a mere portion of that amount (say15-20 thousand) and have someone else cut the grass and/or shovel the snow. Compared to the aforementioned weekly hotel costs, families were able to pay off their timeshare mortgages with about 30 nightly visits worth of the money they weren't able to afford to waste on the pricey rentals. As and end result, they and their children (and grandchildren etc.), hold a deed to vacation for the rest of their lives.

On top of the fact that a family's generations could now vacation for a lifetime, there are two other major advantages to timeshare owners. First, with the airplane's transition from war vessel to public transportation, families could now "swap" their time with any resort in the world. That is something that a snobby neighbor with the big vacation home cannot do. He's stuck in one place until he sells it and buys another.

Also, (perhaps a major reason why our hotelier has turned to an aged Captain Kirk to rent its space through outlets such as Priceline.com) the kitchens in timeshare condominiums allow families a convenience and potential savings that hotel rooms do not. Now, while your snobby neighbor is shoveling two feet of snow off of his walkway this January, our timeshare family is saving hundreds (if not thousands) of dollars by procuring the ingredients for all of their meals at the Stop & Shop (for regional purposes, the grocery store) in Waikiki.

What the Sell is the business model?!

All industries, and the different companies within them, need to bring in more money than they spend on operating costs in order to survive and, hopefully, thrive. Thank you, Captain Obvious! Seriously, though, as all retail businesses need to profit from their endeavors, the philosophical methods in attaining said profit do vary. To me, every outlet in which one shops, to purchase any product or service is a "store." A store is, according to *Webster's*, a retail establishment where goods are offered for sale. Being so, you just finished reading about how social and economic changes have affected the growth of three different types of "goods." We looked at how health and fitness became a good thing. After that, we examined how superior quality, lower-cost, more dependable automobiles from other countries made the U.S. consumer abandon his "buy American" ideals. Finally, we discussed how the many drawbacks of owning second homes and renting hotels fueled the need for and growth of the vacation timeshare industry. Aside from these, there are many other products and services available now, and in the future, that enable aggressive salespeople to earn great livings in their attempt to benefit the lifestyles of others.

The ultimate socio-economic business model, in my not-so-humble opinion, is that of the membership club. Socially, clubs are formed by grouping together people who share similar interests and/or goals. A health club, for example, is formed and supported by hundreds (or thousands) of people who wish have a place in which to exercise. These people may, however, lack the available capital to build and support the facility all by themselves. From an economic standpoint, management/ownership collects fees in the form of "membership dues" in order to support and profit the club. As time goes on, the membership grows, the dues are collected, members get healthier, owner/operators profit, and employees have a great place of employment.

Timeshare, insurance and other groups operate the same way: their members contribute relatively low "dues" in trade for tremendous benefit. A 10-15k dues investment, gives the vacation timeshare owner the equivalent, as any learned resort manager would agree, up to, or more than 100k in vacation value. A few thousand dollars per year in health insurance dues will protect its members from potentially hundreds of thousands of dollars of potential medical bills. To me, the opportunity to join a club is equivalent to the opportunity to trade 10 consumer cents for a dollar of value. If I offered you 1000 dollars in trade for 100, what would you do? How quickly would you make that trade? I love member-based clubs because salespeople have the ability to create nearly infinite value compared a relatively minute investment.

Aside from the value perspective, a "member" has a much deeper contribution to a business than a "customer" does. As they both support the business with the money in their pockets, members share stake in the growth and success of clubs to which they belong. They care that is does well financially so it can be operating for them when they need it. If the club operates up to and beyond a member's expectations, he will refer and recommend other people he knows to use and support it as well. Each member of a successful club will, on average, recruit 1 new member. Retention and renewal rates should also be high because, if the club met member expectations, why would people ever wish to leave the club? When would the health club member cease to want good health? If, on the other hand, the club fails to meet member expectations, referral and retention rates will be minimal, if not totally non-existent. If there are no members, there will be no club.

What the Sell is it worth?

As you can see, social and economic change can be found in many different ways throughout any example of "What the Sell?!" There are a few simple factors for which you can look, that are prevalent throughout the examples I just gave, in your attempt to find the right product or service for you to represent. For one, they are all, in my opinion, very low risk. After all, what is the risk of improving one's health, driving a newer (safer) automobile, or owning affordable vacations for the family? Considering the fact that people blow most of their money one way or another without even really noticing it, what is the real risk of investing the money that is going to be spent anyway? When it comes to the amount of money consumers are able to invest, keep in mind that as time (and inevitable economic downtrends) marches on people will have less and less of it available. A true "What the Sell?!" product or service has to be able to fit into a realistic budget.

Aside from a low (perceived) cost, "What the Sell?!" must offer an extremely high reward potential in return. Just as you aspire to become a (multi) millionaire through sales, your customer should (perceive to) receive a million dollars worth of benefit. If said trade isn't heavily loaded in his favor, he is not going to make it. From that perspective, what price would one put on the self esteem that great results at the health club may offer, the safety and sense of accomplishment that a new car provides or the lifetime of memories created by families on their timeshare vacations? When sold creatively (as I will do my best to show you) the perceived value to your customer of "What the Sell?!" should make purchasing and using it a virtual "no brainer".

The actual quality of the product or service must also be in line with the perceived value you have created while selling it. Throughout time, many sales "gurus" have instructed salespeople to "over-promise and over-deliver" in an attempt to create value. Even so, many customers have complained about being over-promised and under-delivered. Why, you ask, is that a continual problem for salespeople? The answer is as simple as it is crucial: as a sales representative of any product or service, you will always be more knowledgeable and enthusiastic about it than any customer ever will. And, because our incomes depend on it, we sometimes have the tendency to make much more out of our respective products and services than they really are.

In an attempt to keep it simple, I recommend you just "promise" and "deliver". Make sure you sell high value; but only that which your product or service can actually match. Nothing adds to the problems that we face as salespeople like products and services failing to do what we say they will. In other words, put your mouth where the money is.

As we near the end of the "What the Sell?!" section, let me leave you with a few more thoughts: Literally everything that is owned by someone was sold to him by someone else first. This means, whether you believe it or not, you can sell anything you choose to sell. That also means that you have both the right and responsibility to sell something you love. If you are a true enthusiast of the product/service you represent you will always be happy while selling it. Even while you may be miserable about the rest of your life, (I do hope that's not the case) you can always be happy selling what it is you do. If you have to go to meetings or motivational seminars to get "pumped up" enough to make money to put in your own pocket, there is a solid chance that you are selling the wrong product or service for you. It happens. Some (a lot) of the people in sales seem to "end up" there. As little kids, we wanted to play "doctor" or "fireman". Nobody that I knew (including myself) played "car salesman". While some people discover careers in sales through life experiment, others (like myself and perhaps you) understand early on that making money selling (producing) is the only way we're guaranteed to have jobs and remain necessary assets to the rest of society. Being necessary will make you money. How necessary can you become to the furthering of the product or service you sell?

III.   Where the Sell?!: The connection between you and your employer

Every animal needs the proper environment

It was another brutally cold northeast winter morning. On this day, however, the sun actually rose above the twenty foot snow bank outside the window. In other words, it was a beautiful day! With the heat on "high", my girlfriend and I sat on the couch and watched a rerun of Beverly Hills Cop on a brand new flat screen HDTV. During a commercial, I offered to refill her coffee while preparing my cereal. After breakfast, I went to the computer desk to check out ESPN.com. (I'm sure there was some fantasy football information that I just had to find out.) Once I was done surfing the net, I returned to the couch, my girlfriend, and (a very young) Eddie Murphy. It was just about then that the smiling attendant informed my girlfriend that the service work on her car had been completed. Although this place seemed more comfortable than my own home, "unfortunately" the service was finished and we had to leave. Do your customers feel that way about the business you represent? Do they hate to leave? Do they love it enough to include its name (favorably) in the next book they may write? What would it be worth to you and your company to find out? What would it be worth to you if I agreed to stop asking all these questions? Fortunately, the answer is around $10 plus any applicable shipping and handling. (Yes, another bad joke in a somewhat bearable book)

Everyone else can ask the people at Protech Automotive Services in Johnston, RI. It is so clean and hospitable that I am actually looking forward to my next major car problem! (Not really, but I'm sure you get the point.). By creating a "Where the Sell?!" atmosphere, they have eliminated all of the other available auto service options from my mind. When considering today's economic and competitive challenges, they've earned a lot of word-of-mouth advertising and future business at no cost to them. In order to corner the auto service market, they didn't have to do anything except provide "better than home" comfort to myself and others. Doesn't it make sense that a business with a captive audience (waiting customers who happen to lack transportation) should provide the most comfortable accommodations possible for their (paying) customers? In my 20 years of experience in sales, a comfortable customer is a (relatively) happy and understanding customer. Trust me: it is this type of customer that you will prefer dealing with, if, of course, one of your goals happens to be the preservation of at least some of your sanity.

So how can you help create this magnetic type of atmosphere? "Where the Sell?!" workplaces are willing to upgrade their surroundings beyond the normal customer expectations of similar businesses. When I think of auto service centers, the ones that come to mind are typically dirty and uncomfortable, "featuring" old chairs, dusty television sets and (several) vending machines. In some of them, the smoking area is way too close to the waiting area. It's almost as if you need to escape these places as fast as you can with (most of) your health in tact.

We all dread spending extra money on car repairs. Thanks to Protech, (and other forward-thinking businesses) customers no longer have to dread the waiting room experience. Sure, it probably "cost" them a few thousand dollars more to be able to offer the very comfortable chairs, HDTV, computers, complimentary food and beverages. Of course, nobody wants to spend more money than they have to (especially business owners that have to sacrifice their own profits for the cause). However, when you compare a minor sacrifice (like a few thousand written-off dollars) to capture a major portion of the market, making such an investment should be a virtual "no-brainer". What was Protech thinking when they set out complimentary water, soda, juice, coffee/tea, cereal, fruit snacks etc.? It (to me) says "this is your home". Nothing says "you are not a member of this house" quite like a soda machine. Are there any vending machines in your home? There is a difference between investing wisely for the betterment of your company and just being cheap. Those who understand that will be the only ones that will survive in business today and in the future. People have been getting used to "dream environments" for a few years now. Don't let your business become their next nightmare. From a customer comfort standpoint, when we talk about the atmosphere of an auto service station there is that which I described at Protech, and then there is everybody else. They are the best. Who cares about the rest?

While you have expectations of your work environment, you should also have expectations of the people who constitute the workplace: The boss, your peers, other employees and customers. Each of these groups plays a critical role in the success of the company and, more importantly, the padding of your paycheck. Let us examine the roles of these relationships.

Who's "the boss"?

First let's take a look at the most important relationship within the workplace. Whether you sell in-house (store/showroom) or on the road (private homes/offices), you will have to answer to someone. In this book, this person will be referred to as "the boss". Whether the boss is the owner or manager (or both) of your company, he is in charge. The fate (success or failure) of this company is in his hands. He has bigger concerns (in running an entire business) than that of you and your paycheck. If he owns the company, he is the one who takes all of the financial (and accompanying emotional) risk. In my book, that gives him the right to make big decisions and to expect respect and cooperation from his employees when he does. Just like Mom and Dad used to say, it is his house and, being so, you must obey his rules. Unlike the boss, however, Mom and Dad neither pay you to be their kid nor can they fire and replace you with a classified ad. (At least I don't think so.)The decisions that the boss makes, of course, are for the good of the entire company. When it comes to your attitude toward and dealing with him never, ever forget this. Thus ends the "boss butt-kissing" portion of this book.

The aforementioned statements are not to suggest that, sometimes, even the most well- meaning bosses, occasionally do not make bad decisions that negatively affect the business. We all make mistakes. Does your boss (as the person who technically answers to no one) have the ability to recognize his mistakes (or flaws), correct them and grow as a better boss? (He expects you to do the same, doesn't he?) Or, are we dealing with someone who "never makes a mistake" or is "always right"? We have all worked for people like this is the past, haven't we; the people who think that having enough capital to purchase a business automatically makes them "right" in everything they do? The dollar amount in one's bank account only shows the money he has; not necessarily where it came from. From my own experience, I can tell you that good bosses seldom become bad ones, and the bad ones seldom wake up someday and become good ones. Bad bosses are similar to bad economies; they tend to come and go over time. Even if surviving them may seem like an eternity, they certainly don't last forever. Also, they tend to crush their own businesses much like Godzilla (circa 1954, not the Mathew Broderick one) might stomp a Mr. Rogers' Neighborhood-looking Japanese movie set. Economic recessions and gigantic lizard-type creatures are both uncontrollable factors outside the immediate business. Fortunately, both leave many existing businesses standing and operating once they pass. The only way this can happen though, is if the boss is willing to do his best with what and whom he has to work internally. Every effort he makes internally must be done with a focus to hold malignant external forces at bay. How can you help him keep his foundation strong so it can withstand the pressure of the ever mounting external forces he will face for the rest of the life of the business?

Here's an analogy for all of the animal lovers reading this: bosses are like pet owners. If a pet owner loves his three cats (houses, feeds, pets them) the cats will love him back (purr a lot, fall asleep on your chest and occasionally bring you dead mice and birds as "gifts"). On the other hand, some pet owners (physically) abuse their pets. They are cruel to them in ways that turn my stomach. As a result, the frightened pets eventually run away. If the boss abuses his power against his employees, like frightened pets, they will also eventually run away (creating massive turnover). He will then find himself toiling in a lowly-paid never-ending cycle of hiring, training, and firing (as if they were actually a part of his company's daily operations, which they are not). In the end, the boss will be tired, frustrated, and replaced (just like all of the employees he has abused). Also, people, unlike pets, can get together and verbally bash the "stuff" out of the boss behind (or in front of) his back. If that happens, the boss will become "public enemy number one" in his own house! A boss, just like any employee, can be his company's own worst enemy. A large percentage of newer businesses with newer owners and managers fail (miserably) during the infant (-ile) stage of the business for a reason. The "reason" just might be running the business. (Just think "I+Run=RUIN") Just as he loves to take credit for the success of the business, the boss is solely to blame for its failure. That said, a real "Where the Sell?!" boss will first hire, train, and develop the right people. Secondly, and by far more importantly, he will "step aside" and let those people do their jobs. Nobody appreciates a micro-managing babysitter.

You, as an employee, might not like all of the decisions and directions (or lack thereof) made by the boss, but, regardless of your skill level, you are just another (replaceable) "moving part" to him. If you fail to perform your function, like any moving part, you will be replaced by someone who will perform up to and exceeding the boss's expectations.

MUTUAL expectations, MUTUAL respect

What should your employer expect of you as a salesperson? As simple a question as it seems, the answer varies greatly from workplace to workplace. In my experience, this is the single most maddening issue with which salespeople have traditionally dealt. His primary expectations should be that you show up on time (or a few minutes early) and sell his product or service consistently, enthusiastically, and ethically throughout the workday. Whether that means that you are learning your craft (training), prospecting appointments, actually selling customers, or getting referrals, sales is a business of production. The boss (and your paycheck and family) expects you to be productive. Secondarily, he also expects that you be helpful to and respectful of other employees around you. No manager needs a player on his team working against or holding back the productivity of any others on his team. Being helpful, though, neither makes you the janitor nor does it mean you owe the boss "extra" hours because can't figure out how to properly staff the place.

Every successful salesperson, with whom I have had the pleasure of working, basically expects the same two things from their employer: knowledge of the entire job description (not just the good stuff) before he agrees to committing his life to working for this company and; the respect for the ability of the salesperson who will accomplish what the owner/manager either cannot or is not willing to do (move the product or service from seller's workplace to buyers home).

I've always felt that the misrepresentation of a specific job description led directly to the negativity of the salespeople. As positive as you would think salespeople need to be, there are many with outwardly negative attitudes and/or outlooks. It seems like the beginning of every workday is "game over" for them. You know the people I'm talking about, don't you? They are the ones that the boss pointed out to you during the initial tour of the workplace as he said, "stay away from him, he's miserable" (or something to that effect). Every time I heard something like that, I would wonder why these "ultra-talented" bosses kept hiring such negative people. Why would it make any sense, while trying to create a sales-conducive atmosphere, to willingly employ such "miserable bastids"? (I'm from the northeast. That's how we talk.)

Therein lies a huge problem that has faced all salespeople since the dawn of time (or that of selling at least). These "negative" salespeople were once eager applicants (just like you). They spent a great deal of time and energy "selling" the then-prospective boss on their sales ability and eagerness to display it for big paychecks and a solid future (just like you). They carefully listened to everything the interviewer (prospective boss) said about the job description (just like you). After weighing their options, they chose to put their (and their family's) financial future in the hands of this employer (just like you). The relationship began with two smiles, a handshake and a brilliant outlook for the present and future. (I would keep doing this "just like you" stuff, but I'm sure you get the point.)

What created that Bruce Banner – to- The Hulk-like transformation from "happy new guy" (yes, like you) to "miserable bastid" in this particular office? Perhaps the answer lies within the following rant:

"Mr. Employer: I know that it is your name signed at the bottom of my check. However, it is my effort that is solely responsible for the amount I pay myself (via commissions) on that check. Don't look at the small percentage (commission) that I earn (as it exceeds six figures per year), and then tell me that you don't make any money. Don't keep 95% of the money from the deal, give me (a paltry) 5% and try to tell me that I'm the one who is overpaid. I only overpay myself when I overproduce for you. Don't ever try to 'justify' lowering my commission rate, cutting my time off, or adding to my duties by telling me 'how bad everyone else has it' or that I'm 'lucky' to have a job 'in this economy'. Don't ever forget, that if I have the ability to make great money working for you, I can make great money anywhere. You and your business are not alone on a remote island with no competition and no laws. On the contrary, there is so much competition for my skills, that you had better treat me the same way that you demand I treat you. If not, you will become the captain of a soon-to-be sunken ship with no one there to help bail you out. At that point, you will actually wish that you and your business were on a remote island. But, look at the bright side: At least you will be dry!"

My dear reader, if you, at any point in your tenure at any workplace, feel you need to have any or all of the aforementioned conversation (rant) with your boss, my advice to you is to get on that proverbial lifeboat now! No matter how good a salesperson you are, you will never be able to bail out a sinking ship, piloted by a bad captain, all by yourself (which you will have to do because the boss drove all the other good salespeople away). Instead, let the captain go down with the ship. After all, as he reminds you time and again, it is his business, not yours.

All of the animals in the zoo

While a professional relationship, based on mutual respect, is a must between an employer and an employee, it is also a must between the employees themselves. Having sold side-by-side with over a thousand salespeople in the last 20 years, I'll classify them all in one of two groups: there are those who work hard and get paid a lot of money. And there are those who work hard to complain about everyone and everything and get paid very little. The ones in the first group tend to be happy and in control of their own lives. They sell consistently, oblivious to the jealousy and backstabbing of their "teammates". They are generally too busy to notice it and much too wealthy to care. They are just too busy selling to hang out, huddled in a group of "Wendy Whiners" to complain about the economy, the boss, the lack of (company-generated) traffic, or the paychecks and lifestyle of the successful salesperson at the office.

The salespeople I mentioned in the first group tend to use the knowledge that was passed on to them by other salespeople, to help other salespeople improve whenever they can. Although it is not their primary job to develop you, they know that they were once just like you and learned from someone else like themselves. They understand that selling skills both evolve and get passed on to others over time. In short, they are more than willing to share the information that had once been shared with them. That is one of my favorite reasons for writing this book! They also understand that, while they may compete among each other within the business, they all work toward the same cause: the addition, retention and multiplication of paying customers for this business today. Since they know that the success of the business is actually the sum total of the success of all of its moving parts, these people know that achieving success requires teamwork. Everyone who thinks differently is just a miserable bastid.

One final thought regarding your peer salespeople: Be helpful to them and expect them to be helpful to you. Much about selling is based on the efforts of each individual. In other words, nobody earns anyone else's paychecks, just their own. That said, the entire sales force is a team, and should always act like one. Salespeople should always be willing to help each other out, in any way they can (time-permitting, of course) in support of the bigger picture of the company. Splitting commissions with or "spiffing" other salespeople who assist in your efforts to secure a customer's commitment to buy, while it may be generous, is not a law. Over 20 years, I have assisted in thousands of sales without expecting any more than a simple "thank you." Your kindness will find its own way to pay you back down the road. Beware, however, of any salesperson that is only willing to help you for "a fee". People like this make a majority of their incomes by sticking their hands into the pockets of others. If you ever catch someone sticking his hands in your pockets, feel free to break his fingers.

What about all of the other employees of the business that don't survive on a "commission only" basis? All businesses have people count the money, service the customers, take out the trash, etc. Every single one of these people offers an extremely important contribution to the atmosphere and sell-ability (if you will) of the business. Being so, each of them, in some way contributes to the dollar amount of your paycheck. Even though, as a salesperson, you may earn (possibly more than) several times their annual incomes, never forget their importance for a second. On top of that, people who earn $30,000 per year don't want to hear about the "problems" of someone who earns $130,000 per year, so please be aware of the decibel level of any complaints you may have. The positive contributions of others aren't always reflected in their all-too-modest pay plans. Compensation is based on the boss' perception of the value of an individual's contribution to the company. It is easy for him to compensate salespeople with a percentage of the gross sales. On the other hand, it is not that easy to judge the value of an employee who does not have a direct contribution to the bottom line of the business. Sadly, most bosses take this as an opportunity to over-work, undervalue and underpay most of their employees. How many people at the workplace do you hear complaining about their job being too easy and making way too much money at it? Since they, too, comprise your paycheck, my advice is to treat them with the same respect as you would your best customers. After all, they are potential customers also, aren't they?

Getting out of the box to let customers in

Successful salespeople, bosses, and businesses find ways in which to rely on their existing customers for present and future growth. The customer is, after all, the reason you've "Krazy Glued" yourself to a specific product and workplace in the first place. In my view, you've done so much work up to this point, that its time to spread the wealth both literally and figuratively. We have all heard the phrase "it takes money to make money". Many bosses will utter those words, whereas a "Where the Sell?!" boss, will actually back them up. In that way, they are just like everyone else in the world: a lot of people talk; few take action. Is "the boss" willing to put his money where his mouth is? Is he willing to grow the business through its current customers, as opposed to otherwise wasting advertising dollars prospecting total strangers?

For instance, an auto dealer could take the $25,000 per month (or whatever outrageous amount he claims not to spend) he spends advertising the exact same prices as every other auto dealer (that are available to all customers online anyway) and make better use of it internally. He could offer, through his aggressive sales staff, a one thousand dollar bounty for existing customers to refer a friend to buy a car. "Bring your neighbor to me. If he buys, I'll give you 1000 bucks in cash!" While his competition is treading water using the same old ads, his advertising budget will go directly to selling cars. This way, he only pays for advertising when he sells cars, as opposed to paying up front (just like his competitors) and only hoping to sell cars afterward.

When a salesperson is equipped with as powerful a tool as $1,000 in cash, he has great reason and incentive to (excitedly) keep in constant communication with his customer base. For the same $1,000, an existing customer will avidly look to add you more customers. Of course, since you are the salesperson, your customer need only give you names and contact numbers of his referrals. It is your responsibility to "mine the gold" for him. How many leads do you think you could get from existing customers who have already invested in this business, if they see a potential $1,000 per lead? Or would you prefer to continue "spiffing" $50 per referral sale to get absolutely nothing out of it? Many salespeople who offer unsubstantial referral bonuses end up with equally unsubstantial sales results. Would you, as a salesperson, go out of your way to sell a $30,000 car for a $50 commission? Most likely, neither will your customer.

On the same token, is it wise to spend your advertising money on total strangers, when you could otherwise (productively) redistribute it to people who are already connected to the product and the business? For a business owner, this is like adding salespeople that are able to branch throughout the community. Advertising socially through word-of-mouth, is the most effective advertising ever known to the human being. Why not just strive to keep the internally-produced profit reproducing itself internally? (As you may have guessed already, I have not been formally educated in "creative writing".) In the end, your primary hope is that you bind your customers to the product or service in the same way you are bound to it. However, if you are to expect customers to spread the product's usefulness to others as you do, then, just like you are, they should also be duly compensated.

Back to barter basics (for the first time?)

Holding out the possibility that your boss may not redirect his company's advertising dollars every time "some clown writes a book", or perhaps that you are not close enough to him (much farther down the corporate ladder than he) to suggest such an "outlandish" idea, I have another suggestion that has worked extremely well for other creative, aggressive salespeople in the past: barter the value of your product or service with other local businesses. Many businesses (ie: restaurants, salons, health clubs, hotels, etc.) offer services that are most likely used by many of your current and future customers. Bartering is a perfect way to allow them the benefits of those businesses by doing business with you at yours. For example: Two salespeople offer the same car for sale at the same price. However, one of them offers the potential new customer a $100 gift certificate to his favorite restaurant if he buys from him. The other offers nothing extra. Which one of them do you think is more likely to earn the customer's business?

Here's how it works: barters can be negotiated either on the phone or in person. When representing your business to another one, it is important (as in any sale) to speak with the person who makes the decisions (that's right, the boss). When in contact with him, be sure to get directly to the point. He is very busy. His time, as yours, is too limited (valuable) to waste. Your goal is to make it more than worth his time, because it is your intention to motivate him to add customers to his business. Offer him gift certificates at equal value in trade for gift certificates for his business. For example, if you represent a health club that charges $300 per year, trade a one year membership for $300 worth (say 3 @ $100 each) of gift certificates to a business that your member is likely to want to use. In this case, let's say it is a restaurant. The owner of the restaurant receives a one year membership that he can use for himself, raffle off, or offer internally as an "employee incentive". Many businesses cannot afford to give their employees monetary raises. Incentives, however, are no-cost ways for business owners to improve employee morale regardless of the state of the economy. On top of that, the three eventual recipients of his gift certificates would now have a compelling reason to directly patronize his business. As a result, because of you, he now has a one year health club membership, three new customers and new business from everyone else to whom they spread the word. At the same time, how much did all of this really cost him? In real money, a $100 certificate probably runs him $20-$40 (or maybe less). That means he has added the membership, the morale, and all of the new customers for about $60-$120. What smart business person wouldn't jump at a deal like that?

On your end, you have added a brand new member (a source of referrals all on his own) and valuable incentives that you can use to "bribe" other members to bring their friends to join the health club. By "giving up" space to the recipient of your certificate, the certificates he gives you are guaranteed to add at least three new (paying) members while spending nothing on advertising.

Not only do new customers multiply themselves within each initiated barter, but the mutual relationship between the bartered businesses themselves can grow over time. There should be no reason why the businesses can't keep trading products/services for certificates of equal value. Lastly, and not at all the very least, the salesperson who introduces, and successfully manages, a business-to-business barter system looks like a genius compared to all the other salespeople around him.

IV   Who the Sell?!: The connection between you and your customer

The ever-growing disconnect between seller and consumer

Now it is time to take a look at the process of transforming a total stranger into a paying customer and second-tier salesperson. Before we take a specific look at customer connection, it is important to take a look at how buying and selling have evolved over (recent) time. The first step in understanding "Who the Sell?!" will be to examine how the sales arena has changed over time. During my early years, stores were, for the most part, individually owned and operated by local people. Back then, people actually had to go to the store to purchase things. Also, in order to make purchases, they had to deal with live people. The owner/operator/salesperson might have even lived in the same neighborhood as his customers and their families. Being so, he might have even been, to some degree, involved in the personal lives of his customers. There was a strong emphasis on the building of the relationship between the store and its customers. Individual stores tended to specialize in a certain product or service (ie: furniture, appliances.) That meant three things: a lot of stops, limited price comparisons, and many dealings with salespeople. How would it bc possible for one to "comparison shop" if there were nothing else within reasonable reach with which to compare? The consumer's lack of ability to compare prices allowed small stores with low inventories and high overhead the ability to charge enough money per item to easily make profit.

During my teen years, large companies started housing multiple types of products under one roof. Vast arrays of diversified inventories captured large portions of the consumer market that preferred more of a "1stopshop" type of atmosphere. The emphasis on personal-touch service of "Mom and Pop" gave way to the convenience and savings of "Home Depot." Shopping rapidly became "price-shopping" and customer service became extinct. Stores and customers no longer cared about each other the way they once had, but the lines at the registers were long and the prices were good. Salespeople were few and far between and customers were just fine with that!

Today, every product or service on the open market is available right at home. The internet has all but eliminated the need to go to the store by creating a worldwide virtual shopping mall right at the consumer's fingertips. Salespeople have to operate differently now than they did in the past because customers no longer need to deal with them anymore if they don't want to. How does any salesperson expect earn a living when the consumer has the ability to bypass him entirely?

Look at why people "shop" on computers in the first place. For one, the computer gives the facts, without bias. It is truthful. It doesn't care whether or not the customer buys. It has no reason at all to pressure its user and create uncomfortable situations.

The consumer can turn off his computer at any time. He cannot, however, just turn off a salesperson (unless he says "no"). A computer won't push the customer into making bad decisions. It is a way for a customer to protect himself. On top of all that, the internet is so convenient that one could roll out of bed at any hour of the day or night and actually shop in his Spiderman Underoos.

You vs. the computer: Who (or what) wins?

It is, with regard to the changes that technology has brought to buying and selling, that makes "who the sell" so important. There are obvious advantages for consumers today, as the internet has empowered them. The farther we go in time, the more empowered they will become. To date, many "sales dinosaurs" have already died off. Like real dinosaurs failed to adapt over time, sales dinosaurs failed to adapt to a more educated customer. The ones I am talking about are the ones who practice the art of sales by deception. These are the people that, over years of abuse of trust, have all but forced the average consumer to sit at home and hide behind his computer screen. For every reason we, as salespeople, have sent consumers away from us toward a computer, we have to find and hone the ability to bring them back.

In order for a salesperson to "battle" the computer in this way, we must offer to the consumer both what the computer can and cannot. Like a computer, we can deliver information in a non-pressure manner to our customer. Unlike a computer, we also have the ability to connect with the customer as a person, to empathize with him. As safe and controllable as a computer may be, it is not a human being. It cannot share in an individual's thoughts, emotions, or feelings. That is our advantage. As technology continues to take over our lives, one's ability to connect interpersonally will become his greatest asset. People in my dad's generation (back when the television show "Happy Days" was real life) had no choice but to interact socially with other people. There wasn't as much need to stress interpersonal communication in the development of a salesperson because it was the only way business was done. The computer didn't enter Dad's life until he felt he was too old to learn how to use it. Many people of his and my generation are, to be polite, awkward with their knowledge and use of computers and the worldwide web. If that is true, the opposite can be said for present and future generations. They are, and will continue to be extremely adept with technology, yet potentially lacking in interpersonal social skills. Let us now begin to examine how we may be able to better socially interact with others so we can become more influential in our customers' decision-making process. In other words, let's re-connect the ever-growing disconnect.

"Don't touch that dial!"???

Right before going to a commercial during an Olympic event, Hall of Fame sportscaster, Al Michaels, signed off by exclaiming "don't touch that dial!" Throughout the last 35 years of my life, as an avid sports fan, I must have heard him say thing same thing a few hundred times without so much as batting an eyelash. In fact, the very same words were used by most broadcasters. This was not during the, then unimaginable, U.S. hockey triumph over the feared and despised Soviet Union. (We were once at "cold" war with them.) On this occasion, I happened to be watching the 2010 winter Olympics. I don't know about you, but I can hardly remember the last time I actually got off my butt to change the channel, let alone the last time I've even seen a dial on a television set. I also sincerely doubt that Mr. Michaels has recently seen one as well. In fact, about half of his viewing audience may not have even known what the (heck) he was talking about. My 8 year old nephew is able to see three-dimensional images on a high definition television. Whether or not his mother allows him to benefit from this technology remains to be seen, yet, I'm quite sure he has never seen a dial on a television set.

On the other hand, when he was 8, my dad only had a radio. It may seem hard to believe, but broadcast entertainment used to be on radio before people could actually see pictures on the box. The relatively rapid technological changes that transformed radio into high definition television proves that, as people, we enjoy being entertained. Before I go out on a tangent, my overall point is that customers of all generations have different memories and experiences, mindsets and values. In order to effectively connect with a customer, you must be willing to understand these things and sell the product or service from your customer's shoes. Before you sell anything to anyone, you need to know "Who the Sell?!"

My dad, me, my nephew: Do we think alike?

Isn't it bitterly ironic that, the people who are the most concerned with their own survival are also the ones who happen to be closest to death? Think about it. I don't know about you, but when I was a teen and young adult, I treated my body like a garbage disposal. I would eat everything in sight, with absolutely no thought to the potential (unhealthy) ramifications of those actions upon my future self. Who does? Today, at 41, I like many people in that age group, pay much more attention to my daily consumption in hopes of enjoying a better quality of life now and in the future. We just don't think like 40 year olds might think at the age of 20. I would assume I can say the same thing about comparing the mindset and thought process of a 65 year old to those aforementioned ages. At 21 you don't spend your time thinking about retirement. After all, you did just start working. Soon enough, you find yourself at 41, wondering when and if you may actually be able to retire. At that point, you've been at "the grind" for about 20 years or more. When you finally reach age 65, you will most likely lament the fact that you put absolutely no thought or preparation into retirement back when you were 21 while, of course, you are sitting in a waiting room getting ready to interview for a new job.

People of different age groups (for reasons like the above and others) have different issues on their minds on a daily basis. These issues (whether we or they like it or not) will constantly change as they go through life. The ability to share an understanding of those issues will ultimately lend to insight on how customers may tend to take the action or lack thereof in spending their money. Saving money to live is more important to older people than to younger ones. That doesn't mean that older folks won't purchase your product or service. It does mean, however, that the older customer will only purchase if this product or service ranks high on his list of priorities for survival. A good example regards his automobile. Whereas he still has the need to get from place to place he may elect to save money by sticking with that particular car for as long as he possibly can. Conversely, he was probably "turning over" a vehicle every two to three years when a daily commute to work was part of his life as a younger man. Of course, he may have a developing sense of urgency to get on that life insurance policy! (I know it sounds like I'm kidding, but who thinks about life insurance at age

21?) At 21, we are thinking about making enough money (since we've never had any) to buy all the things we want and need so that we may enjoy adult life like our predecessors. We are new in the workplace and have much less experience buying, owning, and using things than older people who have been earning spending money for 20,30 or even 40+ years. Young people do, however, have several new credit cards sitting in their pockets telling them that it's ok to buy everything they see. Be careful!

Having less fear due to the lack of survival instincts, younger people are more apt to take a risk, although they may not have the available means to take that risk. Older people have, for the most part, already taken their share of risks. They tend to play it safe. How safe of an investment is your product or service? How does it protect someone? Err on the side of caution with older folks. Younger people, as they have less life experience, have more of a "show me" attitude with regards to learning new things and taking their own risks. People are eager to learn when they're young, and fearful of what they've learned when they get older. For example, let's look at snakes. I am not suggesting that salespeople are slithering reptiles, although, some most certainly are. When I was young, I used to play with (non-poisonous) snakes. Today, however, if I saw one, I would climb a tree faster than any one of my cats could fathom. Although I have never been bitten or bothered by one, as an adult, I have "learned", through Hollywood stories, to be terrified of them.

Thank you very much, Indiana Jones! Fortunately, I believe that through hard work and trust, I may once again be friendly with snakes. Will you be able to convince your customers that you are, in fact, just like them once you let them peel off your slimy exterior? (You do know I'm kidding, right?)

"Trust me!"

Trust is an issue with all people. It is not given. It definitely must be earned both today and in the future. The lack of trust bestowed upon all salespeople by older folks is a direct result of the horrible mistreatment of them (lying or broken promises) in their dealings with some of our predecessors. These vipers have figuratively (and possibly literally) bitten the hands of those who have so graciously fed them throughout their miserable existences in our profession. By preying on people's dreams of a better standard of living, they have done and said (even while deceitful and untrue) whatever it took to steal their trusting customers' money. Deceiving (scamming) someone for the purpose of taking his money is stealing. It is worse than breaking into someone's home while he is on vacation because these snakes do it right in front of their customer's faces. These types of "salespeople" are lower than low, putrid scum. By stealing from others, they have made the job of benefiting others infinitely more difficult than it should ever have to be. We are supposed to by enriching people's lives, not ruining them.

There is some light at the end of the tunnel, though. An older person will never trust all salespeople, but you can get him to trust you. In order to do this, you had better take your time, look him in the eye, and be truthful. Similarly, a younger person doesn't trust you either. Unlike the older gentleman, though, his lack of trust stems from a lack of personal experience in sales and life situations. Were you taught by your parents to trust all strange places and people? (Yes, you can now blame all of the difficulties you have with customers on your parents.) The younger customer has heard all of that "advice" from his parents and predecessors and, as usual, he will ignore it. Showing my idealism, I implore you to show all people that we, and our products and services, exist only to serve their better lifestyle and/or quality of life. Be genuine. If you can do that, you just might make things a little bit easier in the present and future for your customers, yourself, and the ones who come after you. Please.

If your ultimate end game is to connect your product or service with a new home, you must first connect with the homeowner. When you truly connect with someone, you are seeking to understand him, his needs and desires, as they apply to his better standard of living and/or quality of life. If you do not really connect with him, how could you expect to be able to both interpret his personal needs and be able to offer a reasonable solution to overcoming the problem that put him in front of you in the first place? Let's take a look at how to establish this connection in two ways: physically and verbally.

Get physical!

Let's take a look at what it means to connect physically (in a professional sense). Upon introduction, or the very beginning of the interaction, both you and your potential customer will look each other squarely in the eye and shake hands firmly. While most people will think this is automatic and a minor detail, let's talk about what a simple handshake really means. Isn't it safe to assume that, throughout the course of one's life, he makes physical contact, in the form of either a handshake or a hug, with less than 10,000 people? How does that number compare to the more than seven billion people who, together with you and the other polar bears, roam the earth? Considering the disparity between those two numbers, wouldn't it be safe to assume (for the most part) that the people with whom you've had some sort of physical contact belong in the elite group of those who make up your life?

The quality of your life and your lifestyle has everything to do with the strength of the connections you make with those people. When we think in terms of contact, which is the stronger: that of a casual acquaintance or that of a close friend or relative? That is why a salesperson should be seeking to begin a relationship with the customer as opposed to just selling him something. Would you tend to trust someone that you just met more then someone you have known for many years? Neither does the average potential customer. Fortunately, if you focus on it, you can develop a very close relationship with your potential customer through the different points of connection that you can establish with him. Aside from that, isn't it a lot of fun making friends anyway? Our goal, as salespeople, is to make as many friends as possible and benefit their lifestyles as much as we can with the products that we sell to them. Of course, the hour and half or less that you have to communicate with your potential customer is significantly less time than it takes to build most relationships. That should explain why I just took so much time to explain one minute little detail like a handshake. You don't have a large quantity of time. You need to make sure that what little time you do have is used to achieve the utmost quality.

Now that we have established the importance of physical connection, aside from the aforementioned handshake, how do we create it? Connect on a posture-to-posture basis. When you are looking to connect on a posture-to-posture basis, all points of your posture need to be facing directly toward your customer. Open and direct posture will lead to open and direct communication. When you are an open posture, your eyes and shoulders will be facing your potential customer.

When you have effectively matched the customer's posture, it'll seem almost as if you and he are staring in a mirror. Let's face it, after making a big decision, the only person to whom he'll really answer is typically staring back at him from the mirror. Think about it: When you are considering advice, do you listen more to what someone else is telling you, or to what you are telling yourself? People like to listen to their own advice. Matching his posture will help put you into the customer's shoes. And, as you are leading him, he will feel as if he were leading himself. Now, obviously, customers do not lead us through the selling process. Contrary to the belief of many salespeople I've met, there is no such thing as "customer training school." However, we ultimately want the idea of purchasing to come from the customer (or at least make him think that it did). If his physical response is markedly different than yours (ie., folded arms or a scowl on his face while you are smiling like the cat that ate the canary) he is expressing his disagreement with you. Chances are, he is displaying this disagreement because the pace of your communication is at a different speed than he is comfortable with. Always keep in mind that, in sales, we are constantly seeking agreement. In my experience, the mouth won't agree to buy anything from you unless the rest of the body does first.

From mouth to ears to mouth to ears

Connecting verbally is the way we "signal" the brain to support what the body is experiencing physically. Just like in matching postures, where you are attempting to look "like" your potential customer, verbal connection allows you to think like him. Before you attempt to establish the verbal connection, think about the people in your life to whom you are the closest. These people typically fall into one of two categories: relatives or friends. Being that one hour is not nearly enough time for you to marry into someone's family, I suggest you opt for the relationship of the latter. Make sales by making friends. Most relatives know you much to well you to actually take you seriously anyway, right?

So what is the best way to make a friend? Since you are seeking to establish overall agreement, I suggest you seek similarity. Ask questions that establish common ground between you and the customer. Joke around a little bit. After all, friends joke around with each other, don't they? Have some fun. Show the customer that a salesperson is actually a person, and not just a blood money-sucking vampire. Most transparent salespeople ask a ton of obviously superficial, invasive questions in an extremely lazy attempt get all the information they need to make the sale. In doing so, they forget to show the customer that he is, in fact, dealing with an actual human being. Is that how you make friends? In sales, there is a huge difference between becoming a helpful influence and that of a commission-hungry salesperson who is probing an increasingly-uncomfortable person who will never become a paying customer.

When you have truly established a friendship, both you and the customer will know personal things about each others lives. The both of you should also sincerely care about the direction in which those lives are going. Some of the topics that people use to establish friendship include: shared interests, hobbies, sports fanaticism, work life, family life and future goals. When the potential customer shares those types of things with you, he has effectively accepted your invitation to friendship. He will also be speaking openly and freely as he asks personal and professional questions of you. Just the same as you deal with others, he opens up and asks questions of you if he really wants to establish the friendship.

When, in attempt to connect verbally, you either get negative responses or no response at all, most likely you are just trying to "sell" this guy and not trying to establish a friendship. The sale will come only if the friendship comes first.

What's your name?

Have you ever met someone who named his house, boat, or car? Why is that? Why don't the Duke boys just refer to the "General Lee" as "the orange car with the Confederate flag on top of it"? The answer is simple: When you name something, it becomes yours.

It shows the rest of the world that you are not only close to it, but that you love it. Love is, as most of us know, the strongest positive connection there is in the world. When it comes to a person's child, love transforms "this kid" into "Bobby". While I am not suggesting that you fall in love with your customers, using their names often during your interactions with them will bring the two of you closer. When (if) they talk about you to their friends, would you rather be known as "some sales guy" or "Ted" (if that is, in fact, your name)? When speaking to your customer, do you think he'd rather hear "sir, buddy, or chief etc.) or "Bill"? Acquaintances tend to refer to each other, if at all, informally, whereas friends use each other's names. Since my advice to you is to establish a friendship, I suggest you do the latter, Chief. On a final note, if you think the customer is "dozing off" during your sales presentation, do what the school teacher did to you when you did the same during class (No, don't hit him on the wrist with a ruler): call out his name and see how quickly he wakes up!

Listen up!

One of the most basic, yet integral, aspects of selling is also one of its most overlooked. It is "overlooked" because it is not seen. Unfortunately, many times, the failure to make a sale is the direct result of the salesperson's failure to recognize what he should have heard the customer saying to him. Many customers tell us exactly how to sell them, yet, we are too busy trying to think of the next thing to say, to actually listen to what is being said to us. Being brutally honest with yourself, does that sound (all puns intended) familiar? "Not listening" is a very easy habit for people to get into. Most of us would rather just open our eyes and interpret information visually. When you consider the amount time we spend staring at computer and television screens, isn't it amazing that our ears have not fallen off our heads due to a complete lack of use?

I suggest treating your listening skills like a bodybuilder treats his muscles: exercise them until they get bigger. To accomplish this, approach listening in the same manner in which someone with an actual visual impairment might. It has been said that those with visual and/or other impairments, experience a "heightening" of their other properly functioning senses. If all humans have roughly the same brain capacity, it would make sense that, if one were operating only 4 senses instead of the normal 5, more mental focus could be applied to the remaining senses. While I don't believe the remaining senses are "heightened", I do believe that, just like weightlifting increases muscle strength, intentional listening will increase "hearing strength". In order to develop this "strength", spend some time every day (blindfolded if you have to) listening to something.

"Practicing" listening will not only make you naturally more accustomed to doing it, but it will allow you to "see" the things inside your head that you would normally need to with your eyes. I'm sure, with the obvious risks of both sounding completely insane and prompting you to angrily return this book, you've been able to "see" things in your head that have been described to you by someone else, haven't you? Didn't Grandpa ever sit you on his knee and tell you a story while allowing you to have a sip of his beer? Anyway, shut your eyes and listen closely to something that both interests you and makes you think. Try not to listen to your favorite music while training your "hearing strength", as much of it is already pre- programmed into your memory banks. That would be the equivalent of a bodybuilder lifting the same exact weight over and again. In other words, it'll get you nowhere. I, for one, am a self-professed sports radio addict. (There, I've admitted it!) Although I spend way too much time obsessing about the Red Sox and Patriots, listening to sports radio has had a tremendously positive effect on my listening skills, dealings with customers, and paychecks.

Since you are now focused on listening to your customer, I strongly suggest you enlist the help of a notepad (or, for the technologically adept, "ipad", "kindle" etc.) as well. Speaking from experience, a salesperson's chance of remembering every important detail that has been discussed for over an hour is a slim one at best. Even if your head is somewhat like a voice-activated tape recorder, it is much easier for you to use information that you have written down, rather than hoping to recall it from memory when you really need it. (That is, of course, if you actually wish to finalize the sale) Haven't we all had a restaurant dining experience or two, where the waiter "memorized" all of the orders, only to get some of it wrong? I'm not downing people in the service industry, but the waiter's only job is to bring you exactly what you ordered. It is not, unbeknownst to some of them, simply to suggest the priciest dishes on the menu in order to get the healthiest tip possible. When customers perceive that you are not carefully noting the things they say, they will not invest any further time or income in you. Also, from the customer's perspective, note-taking demonstrates the type of diligence he expects from someone whom he will entrust. If he sees that you care about what he is saying now, he will be much more comfortable opening up and giving you the information you are going to need later.

V. How the Sell?!: Connecting your customer to the product or service

Chart the path to success

As a newer salesperson, this is the section of the book that I would have read first. Perhaps you are doing the same. If so, that would make sense. At this moment, you are already attempting to sell something to someone. You have a job, familiarity with your product, and a customer in front of you. Just exactly how to get from where you are, all the way to that little bit of financial gratification, also known as "the commission", is the most confusing process for most salespeople. In order for you to reach any goal, you must first gain a full understanding of how to get there. What would happen if you attempted to drive from New York City to Seattle, Washington without using a map? What are the odds that you actually reach your destination after driving aimlessly for 3,000 miles? If I were a betting man, as I am not because gambling is, as noted a few times in this book, illegal, I would set those odds at about 1,000,000-to-1. Do you really want to make a million sales presentations before you make one single sale? Even so, throughout my 20 year sales career, I've seen many salespeople attempt to talk to customers for "3,000 miles" and get absolutely nowhere. Let me now provide you with my best version of our map. As I do, however, please do not assume that, by following this "map", you will eventually become a better, more courteous driver. In other words, I can't fix everything.

Survey says???

A great way (excuse) to collect the much-needed information in order to secure buying commitments from potential customers is to conduct some sort of questionnaire or survey. Many successful companies and salespeople employ the use of surveys in an effort to establish open communication with their customers at the inception of their sales presentations. Aside from making the process of establishing a relationship with your customer a heck of a lot easier, surveys give people a chance to voice their opinions. And, as we know, people love to give their opinions. Let's face it: people love to participate in surveys simply because they love to hear themselves talk. It makes them feel as if they have something important to say. Even simpler, it makes them feel important. How do you, my learned reader, feel about that statement? See?

A carefully-crafted questionnaire helps the salesperson discover the potential wants and needs of his customers by allowing them the opportunity to speak openly and freely. With respect to that, if you are designing your own survey, carefully construct questions related to the product or service you represent, your customer's history in this area, and changes he would make to ensure himself better results in the present and future. For example: While selling timeshare, the salesperson may ask his customer about the best vacation he ever took. What did he like most about it? The answer will most likely revolve around spending quality time with his family, exciting new experiences, relaxation and/or other "happy" things. Then, ask what he liked least about it. Aside from the standard nightmares associated with traveling (airport delays, screaming kids, etc.), most people will openly voice displeasure regarding the monetary cost of taking great vacations. Now the big question: "If the money wasn't an issue, would you be willing to take vacations of that, and even higher quality, more often?" Aside from giving the salesperson a resounding and important "yes", that type of question will, most certainly, peak your customer's curiosity regarding the possibility of living a more-fulfilling life through vacation timeshare ownership. Most surveys contain 10 to 20 open-ended questions that will take (depending on the specific type of sale) 15 to 30 minutest to complete. On a final note, the salesperson who introduces the survey into his company's selling process will very likely be known as the "foremost authority" on sales in the place. Admiration, adulation, and alliteration aside, it is a very helpful way to "climb the ladder".

Demonstration magic

Before you depart on any trip consisting of more than 3,000 miles, you must first make sure that you are, in fact, "mentally" prepared for a trip of such magnitude. You need to get into a successful mindset before embarking on such a long, difficult, and potentially hazardous journey. Try this as a mental exercise to get yourself into the proper mindset for your sales demonstration: Think of yourself as a magician who is about to put on a magic show. When you think about it, aren't magicians and highly successful salespeople are very similar? Please allow me to both point out and explain some of these similarities.

For one, the magician puts on a show that is meant to "wow" his audience. If the salesperson's demonstration doesn't "wow" his customer, there will be no sale. The magician will boldly and confidently state the goal of his tricks: "Watch me pull a rabbit out of this hat." Likewise, a salesperson must begin his presentation by boldly and confidently stating his purpose: to introduce and infuse the benefits of his "magical" product or service into his customer's life. Although the magician's audience wants to be entertained, he experiences various degrees of skepticism form them while performing his tricks. On the same token, don't many of your potential customers look for the "strings that are attached?" Being so, it takes a great deal of patience, care and precision for magicians and salespeople to both establish credibility and the believability in the performance of their "tricks". This means that both, magicians and salespeople, need to take the time to build necessary rapport with their respective audiences and perform their tricks with flawless expertise. In order to do that, magicians will often ask a member of his audience to "assist" in the performance. In order to successfully make sales, salespeople must also involve their prospective customers in sales demonstrations. Obviously, great salespeople and magicians need a lot of practice in their trades. Magicians, being people, are also prone to making the occasional mistake while performing tricks. They, like salespeople, always need to be consciously aware of just exactly what step of the process they are in, so they can correct the mistake and move forward. One mistake will not kill your sale. Failure to recognize and correct your mistake, however, will kill the sale. When the proper, pre-planned steps are handled with the care and expertise required, magicians pull rabbits out of hats and salespeople pull sales out of their…Lastly, magicians who can't do tricks can be found in the same place as salespeople who can't sell: standing in the unemployment line.

It is, with regard to the preciseness of the magician's steps, that I recommend pre-writing scripted problem-solving feature/benefit scenarios you can "perform" throughout your sales demonstrations. Seek commitments of ownership and usage as a result of the "oohs and aahs" of these scenarios. You should be able to develop at least 5 to 10 different ones based on the benefits of usage of your product or service. Each scenario should begin with describing an everyday scene. Next, insert any hindrance to quality of life due to non-usage of your product. In other words, what particular problem can we fix here? Then, just like Bullwinkle pulling a rabbit out of his hat, here's the product benefit! Thoroughly, but quickly, explain the upgrade of lifestyle. End the scenario with a confirmation from the customer that ownership and usage is the way for this person to go. "Wouldn't you agree that you and your family would be better off using this product because of this benefit?" After he says "yes", shake his hand to both solidify agreement and deepen the friendship. If you repeat this process successfully 5 to 10 times in a row, you will procure 5 to 10 more "yeses" and handshakes than your average peer salesperson. You will also have, more importantly, earned the right to both ask for and expect to secure your customer's commitment to buy.

Lead customers to the "promised land"

At this point, you are connected with your product like a magician is with magic. You own it, use it, and happily spend your time influencing others to own and use it, too. You are now in a position to allow your expertise in performing magic through positively benefiting the lifestyle and/or quality of life, of a close friend, by connecting him with the product or service. The question we need to answer now is: Why is he going to buy this product or service today? What is the difference between a product or service that someone wants and one that someone owns and uses? What is the difference between him (or you) staring into that 60 inch HD TV screen at the electronics store and staring into that same TV screen at home?

The difference lies within your understanding of people and what they want as opposed to what they need. Everybody wants things. Whether you are a whiny baby who wants a cookie or a whiny adult who wants a 60 inch HD TV, as people, we have always wanted things. And, true to human form, we will always want things. We want these things because using them makes us feel good. Feeling good however, is not nearly enough justification for most people to spend their very hard earned money purchasing things they want. Do you own everything you've ever wanted? Neither does your potential customer. In both today's world and in the future, as is the trend economically, not many people have the money to "splurge" on everything they want. They will however, always be able to justify parting with a small stack of money (which is essentially useless to them in that form anyway) for the things they feel they need. Needs are different than wants because they link us directly to our survival.

Human beings need food, water, and warm, dry environments in order to survive. Astoundingly enough, they do not need big screen TVs or BMW 750s. The key is taking these things that people want and using your expertise and influence to make them feel like they can't live without them. When it comes to spending money, it is easier for people to justify purchasing necessities as opposed to luxuries. Even so, we all know that people purchase luxuries everyday. How do we make a luxury feel like a necessity? While satisfying both needs and luxuries make people feel better, necessities solve or prevent real problems, whereas luxuries do not. For instance, if you do not eat you will not survive. By eating, you have avoided the big problem affectionately known as "death". Wouldn't you agree that either the avoidance of death or pain is a more than suitable reason to part with a little bit of money? The way to turn a want into a perceived need is to simultaneously fulfill the expectations of pleasure of a want and the avoidance of pain of a need.

For instance, in the case of the big screen TV, everyone will agree that a big screen HD TV in the store lends to a substantially better viewing experience than that of the 13 inch black and white model at home. Is that enough to convince a "thrifty" 60 year old man to spend $1500 on the big screen when he already gets the same channels on his current television set? Most likely not, however, that small TV at home combined with his worsening eyesight will make viewing that particular TV, now and in the future, increasingly difficult and possibly even painful won't it? Do you enjoy squinting? Neither does the average 60 year old. On top of that, squinting for hours on end gives people a pretty bad head ache, doesn't it? By the customer choosing to part with that stack of money (that is still doing nothing for him in its current form) in exchange for the new television, he will allow himself a significantly greater viewing pleasure while also significantly decreasing current and potential future physical pain.

Ease the pain

Now, mind you, not all pain is physical. The possibility of avoiding emotional pain will also prompt someone to take action. For example: When someone, who feels as if he is 30lbs overweight, is looking to join a health club, he is making an attempt to alleviate the growing burden on his emotional psyche with regards to the way he feels about his physical state. However, there must be a reason why this person is seeking action today. If that reason were just for purposes of general health, this guy would have started exercising 30lbs ago. In all likelihood, something recently "came up" causing him to dwell on his physical condition much more than he normally does. In my experience, those things typically involve a goal that was set because of a rare occurrence in his life. Perhaps summer may be coming, (he might not have been thinking about it when it started getting cold) maybe he's getting married and has to fit into clothes, or he has an event or a reunion in the near future. If he wants to feel better about himself during any of these or other occasions, he needs to come to a realization that the best course of action is to take action now, and exercise. Nobody ever got into better shape by just "thinking about it". Your goal, as a salesperson, is to find out what exactly is the particular motivation for him to take action today. His life, in some way, is not the way he wants it. He is seeking help from you because he lacks the knowledge and/or discipline to improve it to his liking. The benefits of what you sell, along with your confident guidance, are going to support the customer's motivation to take action today. As a professional, it is your duty to lead him to take that action and infuse the product or service benefits into his daily life.

Sense-ational selling

How much pleasure a person can experience by using your product, likewise, how much pain, either physical or emotional, can he avoid by purchasing it right now? In other words, what enhancements can you help him give himself, and what problem(s) are you helping him solve? If you find the answers to those questions, you are equipped with the information needed to sell this product today. Now that the customer has clearly identified a major problem that he has, it is your job as a salesperson to convince him how using your product or service helps alleviate this pain while allowing him to experience significantly greater pleasure than he currently does. Demonstrating a product is the way we connect the features of this product with the benefits to our customer's lifestyle. So, as you are demonstrating, you are, in effect, transferring the "feeling" of ownership and usage to the customer. If you are doing this correctly, he will clearly see how the ownership and usage of this product serves to better his lifestyle and/or quality of life both now and in the future. If the figurative stack of benefits to his life far exceeds the size of the stack of money for which you ask in trade, he will happily make the trade. Since all salespeople conduct some sort of demonstration, your goal should be to demonstrate more effectively than your peers. Have you ever heard of Houdini? Can you also recite the names of the tens of thousands of other "professional" magicians, whom he made look like the rank amateurs they are?

Effective demonstration is achieved by creating physical and emotional sensation. Just as you would "jumpstart" a dead battery in the winter cold with a fresh jolt of electricity, you should use the usage and benefits of your product to "jumpstart" the customer into taking action today. Without more-than-adequate stimulation, there can and will be no cause for the customer to take action. Would your dead battery start without that jolt? Yes, customers are like dead batteries: they need "jolts. I suggest that you create the positive feeling of sensation, and then allow the customer to justify the feeling through his own rationalization. In order for us to achieve this, let's examine how sensation and rationalization play their parts in the selling process.

In order to create sensation, you must first stimulate one or more of the five physical senses. Please bear with me as I take a mental trip back to grade-school science class. (By the way, I have yet to prove to anyone that I am, in fact, smarter than a fifth-grader.) By stimulating the senses of sight, sound, smell, touch, and taste, we are sending signals from the outside environment directly to the brain. Then, we leave it up to the brain to interpret feeling throughout the body. For instance, when your finger touches a hot coal in the fire, the brain reacts by "telling" your sense of touch, "that hurts like (heck)! Cut it out!"

Being that you are in control of how you stimulate your customer's senses, you are, in effect, in control of the signals that will be sent to his body. For example, wouldn't you agree that we are in control of applying antiperspirant to your armpits? Would you also agree that the signal sent to a customer's brain will be significantly different whether or not you have applied said deodorant? What signal does it send to you (or how do you physically react) when someone smells good? On the other hand, how do you react, both physically and emotionally, when someone smells like they just climbed out of a dumpster? Do you feel the same way? Do you make the same face? Neither does your customer. A pleasing aroma leads to a pleasing environment, which lends itself to a state of agreement. Conversely, a displeasing aroma will, most likely, lead to a state of disagreement, if not disgust. The point is that the signal is going to be both sent and received whether we like it or not. In order to become a highly successful salesperson, you need to put yourself and the customer on the positive side of the senses as much as you possibly can.

Since we have already discussed the importance of smelling good, let's take a look at the other senses that require positive stimulation in order for customers to take action now. What we see in front of us will, most likely, be the first indicator of whether this is a positive or negative environment. That is why, for example, an auto salesperson is always "clean and pressed", well shaven, and his hair (if he still has any) is properly combed. It would also explain why both the dealership he represents and the car his attempting to sell, are immaculately clean. An environment that looks good is one that is conducive to selling.

Now, of course, nobody ever bought a car without driving it first. On that note, it is amazing to me how many times I have witnessed salespeople trying to negotiate the price of a vehicle with customer who has yet to test-drive it for himself. How could a customer ever develop the feelings of ownership and usage, without ever having used it? The physical involvement of touch, as it applies to the usage of a vehicle, sends a signal of empowerment to the brain. How does your customer's heart race when he starts to rev the engine? Simply looking at a car only allows someone to think about using of it. Thinking about things is not a form of action. Feeling empowerment, however, will lead people to take action as long as they are assured that, by doing so, they will be able to maintain that feeling. Of course, as you should constantly keep the customer aware, that continued feeling can only be maintained a result of him purchasing the product or service and using it on a regular basis.

When considering the importance of sound, how do you think that listening to the high-tech sound system in the new car feels to your prospective customer compared to that of the 5 to 10 year old technology currently built into his old one? How does his favorite station sound now? Wouldn't he rather experience this degree of sound quality now and in the future? On the other hand, how does absence of sound due to the solid construction and advanced technology of the new vehicle improve his concentration while driving? Won't the elimination of distractions, such as wind noise and vibration, allow him to better concentrate on his driving, thus allowing him to reach his destination more safely and securely?

Lastly, how is taste applicable to selling a car? I mean (said like Seinfeld) you can't eat the dashboard can you? Have you ever walked into someone's place of business and seen a bowl of candy on the desk? Do you know why it's really there? It's there because, after three hours of meeting with you, both you and your potential customer are famished. Now, while it's ok for you to starve, I would prefer, at this point, to have my customer focused on buying today, not where he's getting his next meal. A little sugar burst may just be the jolt you both need to get this deal done now. Being that survival is always on his mind, a customer will opt to satisfy his hunger over your need to sell every time. Having a little bit of food and coffee may be the difference between you being able to afford to eat or go home broke and hungry.

Here's a quick little quiz to see if you are following me so far: It's 25 degrees outside and you are about to show a car. Do you A.) Drag your freezing customer through the freezing car lot and put him into a freezing car? Or B.) Allow the customer to relax in the warm, friendly environment of the pristine showroom while you retrieve and warm up the vehicle? From a feeling standpoint, which scenario is more likely to lead to the sale of that vehicle? Under which scenario are you providing a greater service to your customer your dealership and yourself?

Is it the money? Make it about the money!

Unfortunately, the feeling of pleasure and the avoidance of pain are usually not pressing enough to part an individual with his hard-earned money, even though he may think he's better off doing just that. He must first find a way, within himself, to justify it to himself and others. How can we, as salespeople, help him accomplish that? How can we make sure that, when he leaves here today, he's made the best decision for himself? If your goal is to help him justify the continuation of the feelings you've helped him create, you need to appeal to his rational side. Rationalization is the brain's way of coming to a logical conclusion that taking action now is the best idea it has to increase the odds of quality survival.

Always keep in mind that, while the body wants to feel good, the brain is always focused on self-preservation and survival. Because of that, the two sides are typically in constant conflict with each other. For your purposes, you need to get them to work together. Here is an example of how rationalization can help support the sensation and justify a purchase. Let's look at the big screen TV that we discussed earlier: Although viewing pleasure would be increased and squinting would be decreased, is that enough to cause a person to part with $1,500 to purchase one? Maybe it will. However, in a "yes or no" world, "maybe" just doesn't exist. In order for us to sell anything to anyone all signals both emotional and logical need to point to yes. To accomplish that, I suggest you hit the customer where it hurts the most: right in the pocket!

First, let's "spread the wealth" a little. A customer's positive decisions also have a significant impact on others around him. Who else, among this customer's family and friends, will derive pleasure and avoid pain by viewing the big screen TV? In my experience, people are more willing to take positive action when it also enhances the lives of others for whom they care. In other words, if he does this, his whole family wins; if not, they lose. When presented with the options of his family losing or winning, which do you think he will prefer? Let's assume that he is really leaning toward the purchase, but parting with the money is holding him back. If that is the case, I would recommend that you offer the customer a simple comparison based on the value of money. For example: People purchase big-screen TVs in an effort to create a "movie theater experience" at home. Aside from the fact that movie theaters now charge $5 for a simple drink of water, it costs more than $20 in "rent" for two people to be able to enjoy less than 2 hours in front of a big screen. Let's assume that your family watches only 2 hours of television per day. (Yeah, right!) As you examine this on a cost-per-use basis (30 bucks per couple, per view), the big screen TV compared to the same experience in the theater would pay for itself in about a month and a half. If you don't believe me, feel free to do the math for yourself.

Being that many of us either own or have considered purchasing HDTVs, please spend the rest of this exercise from the customer's perspective. How much money would you save by purchasing the TV and watching movies at home, instead of at the theater? The comparative amount of savings over time would be astronomical, wouldn't it? How does that month and a half of paying for the TV compare to the free and clear ownership and usage for the rest of the lives of you and your family? That sounds like a very small immediate financial sacrifice in trade for a lifetime of benefit doesn't it? Along the same lines, we could compare one year of going to the movies with watching that movie theatre quality HDTV screen in the comfort of your own home. Over the course of a year, the movies would cost you around $7500 compared to the $1500 it will for you and your family to experience the same (or better) quality viewing at home. The great thing, under the less expensive scenario, you can actually stay longer than a couple of hours!

Here's the same type of comparison as it may apply to selling cars: A dealership customer, who owns the 5 year old car with 50-60K miles on the odometer, has pulled in for service. You, being a highly-aggressive, service-minded, cost-conscious salesperson, take his service bill and easily show him that it regularly costs $2-$3,000 per year to maintain older cars with expired warranty protection. In the next five years, that's $10-$15,000 that he will take out of pocket to spend on the old car, for which he has already paid. At that point, he will own a car that is now 10 years old and still out of warranty protection, with 100K+ miles now on the odometer. This car will now be worthless to him or anybody else to whom he may now wish to sell it. Is that, ultimately, the best situation for him to be in? Unless he has no regard to the value of money, it certainly is not. The astute and aggressive earner you are, you will show your customer how to "mentally" apply the $10-$15,000 he will most definitely spend on his 10 year old car as an investment in the brand new one he and his family really want. Not only will you help him get out of the old car and into the new one, but you are likely to add him a ten year/100,000 mile warranty which, in effect, solves the original problem he had when you first met him in the service area. If that doesn't make you both a well-earned commission and a friend for life, I don't know what will.

What if we were to apply this to an intangible sale, such as a timeshare condominium? While conducting the survey with your potential timeshare owner, find out how much it cost him to take the best vacation he and his family had ever taken. After he admits to spending in between $5,000-$10,000 (or worse, more), ask him how many more vacations of that magnitude he and his family are planning to take in the future. The average wage earner (who, by the way, is your best timeshare candidate) will likely tell you that spending that type of money to go on vacation simply isn't in the budget. It was, most likely, a one-shot deal "dream" vacation. Being a "dream" to most families living during the challenging economic times of today and tomorrow, chances are, considering the ever-rising cost of paying for them, he is not likely to see himself and the family taking a vacation requiring that type of financial commitment ever again. What if, however, as the astute and aggressive earner you are, you were to ask him (as I touched upon in "survey says?") that, if the cost wasn't an issue, would he be willing to take his family on "dream vacations" every year. If money really wasn't an issue, what kind of family-oriented human being wouldn't want to take truly awesome vacations, at least one week of every grueling year?

Whether or not people actually get away one or two weeks per year, most of them will usually find a few weekends, here and there, upon which to "get away". If he were only to admit to getting away just three weekends per year, @$200 per night, he would be spending $1200 per year (plus meals), while at the same time cramming his entire family into one single hotel room. Coincidentally, the same $1200 per year that rents him nothing but "aggravation," may be enough money to cover the annual amount it would take to pay off the investment of his new timeshare condominium. Aside from now owning his vacations, he has also added a money-saving kitchen and some much-needed space for the family. As a result, he and his family may now enjoy the dream vacations they could never afford to take before by investing money they were spending all along. Over the next 20 years of dream vacations, he will save about $85,000 (or much more!) compared to the cost of taking them before he met you. Again, if that doesn't earn you a friend, I still don't know what will.

Some (many) people pretend that, not only do they not have "expendable" income, but they, in fact, carefully monitor every penny that does get spent. Try not to "buy" any of that, as it is, most likely, a lie. The fact is that, even in small increments, we all have money we spend that could otherwise be used somewhere else. For example, if I had a dime for every person who, while smoking a cigarette and drinking coffee, told me that he didn't have "extra" money to buy anything, I would be a very, very wealthy man. Why, you may ask, is that? Well, 1 month's worth of 8 dollar smokes and 3plus dollar coffees (equaling $11 per day) tells me that this customer has at least 330 "extra" dollars to spend every month. I've spent 20 years of my life selling health, timeshare, consumer club memberships and automobiles. And, in my experience, 330 bucks per month will easily buy something worthwhile from each of those categories. In other words, don't take "poverty" as an answer! I mean, however, absolutely no disrespect to the genuinely impoverished. My point is that, as it has been proven for eons, people will make small, short term sacrifices if they see significant benefit to the longer term of their lives. If that statement weren't true, why would anyone (including me and you) ever choose to meet with a salesperson if he didn't really have to?

If my memory serves correct

Whether the product you represent is tangible (able to be touched) or conceptual (an idea), a "mental picture" of ownership and usage must be created if you want to sell it to anyone. People are able to see and touch tangible products, which makes it easier for the product, itself, to create the feeling of sensation. For instance, we can see and touch a TV, a car, a house, and any other physical product. How would "seeing and touching" come in handy during the sale of an insurance policy? In the case of timeshare, one purchases time and space, yet, not a particular time or space. In these, and other types of conceptual sales (ie: club memberships), salespeople have to get creative in their attempts to create enough positive sensation in order to make sales. Keep in mind that, if there is no feeling, there will be no cause for action. How do we create sensation in the absence of a physical product?

My advice to you is to rely upon the positive memories of your customer's past, and connect them with the way he wants to live now and in the future. Let's examine our timeshare condominium for example. What are your customer's favorite memories of great vacations he has had in the past? By asking him that question you are allowing him to create a positive environment within himself. Since you can't see his vision for him, help him better see it himself. Aside from being able to enjoy these same things himself, how does it make him feel to extend that gift to his children and, perhaps, even his grandchildren? Is your grandchild more likely to remember the $50 gift card you got him for his seventh birthday or a trip to Disneyworld? Which of those two scenarios will more likely create lasting memories between grandson and grandfather? In the case of selling a new car, ask him if he remembers the "new car feeling" he had when he bought this one. If money wasn't an issue, would he want to feel that way again? In the case of the health club membership sale, does he remember how he felt when he was in the best shape of his life? Would he be willing to part with a few dollars per week to recapture that feeling? How do you feel about the fact that spending only 10 bucks on this book put you in complete control of your financial future? (Ok, maybe that's a stretch!)

How about another one just for fun? In your mind, can you picture a McDonald's quarter pounder with cheese? Can't you see it so well that you are actually beginning to salivate? I'm getting really hungry now! There are many examples that you can use from someone's past experiences to set up a mental and physical feeling that will be conducive to change, in the form of purchasing your product or service today.

Seal the deal

Asking for the customer's commitment to buy is the equivalent of applying Krazy Glue to the sale and seeing if it sticks. Did you create enough of a bond in your attempt to connect the customer to the product? What's this magician pulling out of his hat: a rabbit or a piece of lint? As a newer salesperson, the attempt to secure a customer's commitment to buy was, by far, the most unnerving part of any selling situation. Why not? "Yes" meant a new customer and paycheck, whereas "no" meant it was back to the phones to make more appointments. Which of these results would you prefer? It never did make sense to me, when at the end of a sales presentation, a customer ended up turning the offer down. It was especially mind-blowing that, throughout the entire presentation, the same customer agreed (time and again) to the specific benefits of ownership and usage of this product would make to his way of life. Why, if the money invested seemed minute compared with the benefits of the product, would anybody not buy this?

It was just so contradictory that it would drive me crazy, which, apparently to some, is not that long of a journey!

In order to preserve my (apparently self-professed) sanity, I had to find a way to solve this problem. I decided to take a close look at how I was asking "commitment" questions. Throughout my entire sales life, mentors and peers told me to get as many "yeses" as I possibly could in order to secure sales. The theory behind it was that, getting customers into the "habit" of saying "yes" during the presentation, made it easier for them to say "yes" to becoming buyers today. In my experience though, people are extremely resistant to saying "yes" when asked to make any type of decision. Why is that? The answer, I believe, has to do with survival. What did "Mommy" say when you reached your hand out to the hot stove burner, the cookie jar, or the pigtail on your sister's hair? In my house it was "No, no, no!" By saying (screaming) "no", she was trying to keep you safe from getting burned, fat, and in the case of pulling sis' hair, having any fun whatsoever. "No" keeps us all from getting burned. (And I do mean by salespeople) "Yes" on the other hand, is an allowance of risk. What would her answer be if you asked "Mom" if you could parachute from a plane at 30,000 feet? "Yes" would have a life or death risk, whereas "no" would keep you safe on the ground. Customers in buying situations say "no" in an attempt to maintain their safety when saying "yes" seems too risky.

The real question is: How can you secure a commitment to buy without getting a "yes"? A commitment, as defined by *Webster's Dictionary*, is something that is bound as if by promise. Instead of asking him if he will buy, ask him why he is promising to buy. Have you ever heard of the term, "choose between the lesser of the two evils"? I believe in the exact opposite when in comes to obtaining buying commitments. When forming a buying commitment question, have your customer choose between the greater of two goods. Choose the two benefits that you feel are most important to your customer per what you have learned about him so far. Then, give him the choice of the two options, which both result in his commitment to buy. For example: "Are you joining this health club today because of the fact you will have more energy or because you will look better in a bathing suit this year? He will either choose one of the benefits or he will hesitate in some way. If he chooses to hesitate at this point, rather than purchase, he is either clearly uncomfortable with the value of the trade or hesitant to make changes in his life. He has either not been properly "sold" on the lifestyle benefits attached to ownership and usage of this product or service, he might just need a little time for the benefits to "sink in". This is where I may differ from other sales training resources that you may have read. In fact, I once read a book that featured more than 20 different "closing techniques", all with "cute" names, that, in my opinion, accomplish nothing more than point out to the customer that he isn't very intelligent. Believe it or not, securing a customer's commitment to buy can be achieved by holding a intelligent conversation, rather than memorizing and using "cute" little tricks.

While it is always the proper mindset to assume the customer is eager to buy at the end of the demonstration, it is also quite understandable that he may see cause to hesitate. If he does, find out what exactly is causing his hesitation. Regardless of the excuse, it's "the money". As a matter of fact, most, if not all, of your (paying) customers have experienced the same type of hesitation or concern. However, upon reflection and re-evaluation of the customer's stated agreed upon lifestyle benefits, most people find that they value the overall upgrade in lifestyle and/or quality of life more than the minor monetary investment it takes to attain either one or both . Wouldn't you agree?

The aforementioned process of isolating and overcoming purchasing hesitation will either lead you to securing a commitment to buy from a soon-to-be-multiplied new customer or a non-paid end to this meeting.

If he elects to buy, congratulate him on the positive change he's made for himself and his family. Also, thank him for choosing you and your company to assist him in the positive change in his lifestyle and/or quality of life. Most products or services have a least a few different payment options. Simply explain them to your customer, and ask him which option is the best one for him to get started on today.

Use the following question in these and any situation you can: Which do you prefer? For example: "We accept credit cards or personal checks. Which do you prefer?"

"Do I have to make a decision today?"

A career in sales certainly provides its share of challenging situations. However, nothing is more off-putting to a salesperson than a customer's steadfast reluctance to make a "decision" whether or not to purchase what he sells. How is it possible that, after an hour or more of your time, the customer's attention, and full disclosure of the facts about the product/service in question, he is unable to make a decision regarding ownership and usage? At least "no" is a definitive (although unacceptable) answer. The very idea of it upsets me so much that, if I hadn't dealt with it more than 20,000 times, I would have gladly omitted it from the book. The truth is, as surely as the sun rising in the east and setting in the west, you will deal with people's indecisiveness every day. Your success in sales will be in direct ratio with your willingness to accept, embrace, and overcome the indecision of others. In order to do that, let's take a look at people, decisions, and your role in bringing them together.

First of all, decisions are made for people, not by them. Choices, on the other hand, are made in an effort to act upon pre-determined decisions. Even though it's only 8:00am, I can already give you a few examples: For one, at 6:00am, my body made the decision to wake up. At that point, I had the choice of either getting out of bed or hitting the snooze button. I chose to get up. The human body needs to be physically fit in order to function properly. Being so, I had the choice of either sitting around on my butt or going for a run. I chose to run. Soon after, my growling stomach, acting on its decision to survive, loudly suggested that I eat breakfast. Even though there are multiple food options, I chose to eat eggs and a bagel. Lastly, my bills decided that I should choose do some writing instead of just staring at the walls.

When your customer has chosen the better option (life with the product or service) in each scenario of the demonstration, he's made the decision that his life would be better if he were to use the product or service. At that point, he's left with a choice: As he goes forward, does he stick with the status quo or does he choose to better his lifestyle and/or quality of life by owning and using said product or service? Smart people have such a need to give the right answer to questions that, if they aren't sure that they're 100 percent correct, they tend to fall into state a mental paralysis. In fact, the smartest person I've ever met is also the most indecisive person I've ever met. Whiny, lowly-paid under-producers deal with quite a few "idiots who can't make a decision."

As a professional salesperson, it is your job to assume a role of leadership by both guiding the customer to the right choice and helping him make it.

If he hesitates, explain to him that it's perfectly understandable that he chooses be cautious when making important life changes. In fact, all of your customers feel the same way. However, if he's been agreeing with you the entire time, he's already made the decision to change his life for the better. You are just offering him a choice in how to accomplish the task. Does he prefer to stay the same or make his life substantially better than it is, today?

As far as the "today" issue goes, I suggest you look at it from three important perspectives: the customer, employer and salesperson. The customer's goal is to improve his life. When given the choice, how will he reach that goal the quickest: starting tomorrow, next week, next month, or today? The employer has invested advertising dollars, a salesperson's time and, most likely, office space in this meeting with the customer. When do you think "the boss" would like to see a return on that investment? (Please use the same choices as before) Lastly, if the timing of the purchase wasn't important, what incentive would there be for the salesperson to try his hardest every time "up"? Many successful sales organizations believe that "there is no 'tomorrow'". Now, my astute reader, you know why.

If, at the end of everything both you and the customer have experienced together, he doesn't want to make a decision, simply ask him what decision it is that he thinks you are asking him to make in the first place. Has he decided that the product or service isn't right for him and his family or is it "the money"? If you've done your job as a salesperson, it's the money. It's alllllways the money! Use the many agreed-upon benefits of the product or service to "funnel down" any and all excuses to money. Then, ask for the customer's commitment to buy again. Repeat this cycle until he gives it to you. If that doesn't work, call the boss over to the table and have him start earning his money!

"The Price is Wrong"

Before I spend a little time giving some advice on how to handle the negotiation of the sale of your chosen product or service, please allow me to clarify the role of a salesperson in negotiations in general. The biggest mistake I've ever seen salespeople (myself included) make, while attempting to negotiate the sale of a product or service, is to introduce and/or involve its price or specific payment into the equation. Let me be crystal clear in this: the price and/or payment of the product or service have nothing to do with the fact that your customer should own and use it. He should own and use it because it significantly benefits his (and his family's) lifestyle and/or quality of life. The price of the product or service is simply the cost of doing business and nothing more. As is it the cost of doing business, everyone who purchases it pays the financial cost associated with it. If I were to use the aforementioned examples from my own professional life (health clubs, cars and timeshares), I would say that customers don't lift prices, drive prices, or vacation on prices; they lift weights, drive cars and vacation on tropical islands. Since I'm sure you see the differences, it is your objective to make sure your customer does as well.

On top of that, most salespeople don't even have the authority to adjust product or service prices however they wish. If they did, two things would surely happen: products and services would cost (next to) nothing and salespeople would make (extremely) healthy commissions after the point of sale. As far as "price" goes, the specific one for your chosen product or service was not only set by the company you represent but, if the company reps manage to sell any of them at all, it is most likely a fair one for all parties involved. If not, the "powers that be" will either make the necessary adjustment in price or go out of business. Hopefully, as far as you are concerned, it isn't the latter.

Having gotten all of that out of my system, I will now offer some (helpful) advice in dealing with the negotiation of a sale. First and foremost, there are two sides in every negotiation. In this case, they would be, of course, you and the customer. Secondly, in any negotiation, both sides are trying to gain something. In this case, you are trying to gain your customer's money and he is trying to gain the product or service at the lowest possible cost to him. (Yes, I realize that I just spent two paragraphs downplaying the "money" aspect of things, but just bear with me.) Thirdly, and by no means least importantly, each side needs to offer something to the other one to make the deal possible. The customer, of course, needs to offer his hard-earned cash to make the deal happen. Since we have already established the fact that there are two sides here, you also need to offer something in order to make the deal happen. The question is: how do you, as a salesperson, with no flexibility in the specific pricing of the product or service, "fight fire with fire" with the customer when he wants "a better deal"? The answer is not only simpler than you think, but it is also a recurring theme throughout this book.

Ask any firefighter if I'm telling the truth. I'm quite sure that, when asked, the firefighter would advise you to fight fire with water. Just as it makes no sense to a fireman to battle a blaze by adding more fire to it, it makes no sense for a salesperson to "fight" the customer's desire to argue "price" with either arguing about or attempting to lower the price of the product or service he represents. My advice to you, whenever the customer attempts to fan the flames of price, would be to douse each attempt with a lifestyle and/or quality of life benefit, and then ask for (and expect) his commitment to buy. If instead, you choose to fight fire with fire by arguing price with price, you will likely accomplish nothing other than (figuratively) burning down your house.

How do you spell "relief"? T.O.

Any baseball fan can tell you that games, like nights at the local bar, are often started by one pitcher and finished by another. Because hurling fastballs can quickly tire out any pitcher's arm, the "starter" may begin to struggle, therefore failing to produce outs as time wears on. If (and when) he tires, he is then "relieved" of his duties by a fresh pitcher. Once inserted, the relief pitcher will bring the needed energy and focus to finish the game. Baseball is, after all, a team game. When the team wins, the starter, the reliever, and the rest of their teammates receive credit for the victory. Regardless of any competitiveness within the team, the immediate goal is for all teammates to do their jobs in an effort to win.

The process of finishing both baseball games and sales are very much alike. (Except for the uniforms) Many sales are "taken over" and completed by someone other than the original salesperson. In fact, in many sales types of sales, it is extremely rare that a salesperson goes through the entire selling process without enlisting the help of, at least, someone. Whether it is a manger, fellow salesperson, or other internal employee, there is always some sort of resource upon whom he can rely to help him get through any sticking points that may ultimately impede the customer's ability to benefit from his product or service.

Your ability to understand how and when to employ "T.O. managers" will greatly enhance your odds of successfully selling any product or service. The first thing you need to identify is just where you happen to be stuck. Is it a price/payment, customer connection, or a lack of understanding (benefits-wise) issue? Or perhaps, is the customer a little tired of hearing it all from you? All of these things happen at times to the best salespeople I've ever known. They, however, understand both where they are in the process and how to employ others to help them move forward.

Communicate your "sticking point" to someone who can help. Managers get paid directly off of the "backs" of their salespeople. When in doubt, always seek the aid and advice of your manager. A capable manager can step in either in person or on the phone and secure commitments from customers who have, up to this point, been properly sold. If proper steps have not been taken by the primary salesperson, no one will get this deal done.

When introducing a manager or someone else to take over a sales presentation, it is important to both show enthusiasm for the new customer and bridge rapport for the person taking over. In the presence of both the T.O. manger and customer, happily state the customer's desire to own and use the product or service to the manager. Then set common ground between the T.O. manager and customer. For example: "(T.O. name), Jesse and Angelika really want to become timeshare owners, but they're a little concerned about 'the money'. Is there any way that you may be able to help? Jesse is also a big Red Sox fan, just like you…"

If you handle it that way, the T.O. manager can quickly raise the emotion back to the proper mood-level that is conducive to buying. Once he gains some friendship and trust, he can use his expertise to ask questions that may eventually lead to securing the sale. In order to be effective, the T.O. manager must duplicate any untaken steps in the order that they would normally appear during any selling situation. Since the fact-finding and demonstration process should have already been done by you, he needs to build his own rapport with the customer, and then secure the sale.

Also, once you've enlisted the help of your T.O. manager, please do him, the customer, and your paycheck a huge favor: Shut up! Let the manager do his job and finish the sale. Nothing is more distracting and detracting than someone interrupting the sales process. Although, it is extremely difficult to sit by, while someone else does your work that is the proper professional courtesy you need to extend to the T.O. manager who is trying to make you money. In other words, have you ever seen a since-replaced starting pitcher reenter the same game?

Before you give up a lifetime of direct and indirect (referral) commissions from this customer, either get a T.O. or lose the game. A losing pitcher doesn't want to "hear it" from other players, the owner, or the fans of this team. Do you? Get a T.O.!

Perhaps, as an end result, your potential customer prefers to walk away without having purchased your product or service. Yes, my dear reader, I am talking about the dreaded "missed" sale: that wasted, non-paid, hour and a half of your life, plus any and all of the prospecting and appointment making that went into it, that makes some sales days longer and downright miserable than they already are. No self-respecting salesperson will ever find enjoyment in any "missed" sale. As awful as they are, however, "missed" sales are as much a fact of selling life as are "made" sales. Being so, a professional never expresses outward derision at the end of any unsuccessful sales presentation. True professionals stay focused on the task at hand, whatever it may be, throughout all of their losses and wins. While it may feel natural, as a human being, to feel let down after a "missed" sale, and it may feel natural to lash out at someone who let you down, it is both unprofessional and, for that matter, "un-adult" to ever show such weakness to a potential customer. Biting remarks or comments that expose any type of "sour grapes" attitude cannot ever be made during any interaction with a potential customer. You don't really want your customer's last impression of you and your business to be a bad one, do you? When you try to rationalize "missed" sales for yourself and your sanity, never lose sight of the responsibilities of both parties involved in any selling situation: Your customer's only responsibility is to allow you his undivided attention (no phone calls or texting) during the allotted time to which you both agreed. It is not, however, at any time, his responsibility to buy from you. If he has fulfilled his obligation, the customer deserves the same level of respect while parting ways, as he did during the initial meeting.

I love to see my customers, except when…

And now, my dear reader, we are entering the part of the book that I dislike the most. (That is why I stuck it near the end.) Someday, when you and your over-extended lifestyle can least afford it, a customer will attempt to return or cancel the product or service you spent so much time and effort infusing into his life. Nobody wants to see the result of his hard work walk back in the door as if none of it mattered at all. Not many things in life hurt more than having to "mentally erase" the freshly-earned dollars in your bank account due to cancelation. Like it or not (and you will not), cancelation will happen some (hopefully a very small percentage) of the time. It seems as if it has taken me 20 years to accept that fact, yet, I still have a difficult time accepting it. Perhaps, many of you reading this feel the same way.

What will make or break you as a salesperson is how you choose to deal with the customer who wants his money back. What I have seen by salespeople in the past, what the customer expects, and what I don't recommend is arguing against the wishes of the customers. When a salesperson makes a sale, he feels that he is both owed and entitled his commission. Being that we are highly reluctant to give back "my money", the natural tendency for salespeople and managers is to try to "convince" the dissatisfied customer to keep (and pay for) the unsatisfactory product or service. Nothing angers customers more than someone else holding their money hostage. How would you feel if you were in the same position? News flash: every customer expects every salesperson to give him big- time b.s. in these situations as he attempts to prove the customer wrong.

My advice to you: give the money back without hesitation or question. If your customer doesn't feel as if you and your company have earned his business, you haven't. You have to keep in mind that, at this point, the customer feels like you've "taken him for a ride", "sold him down the river" or any archaic phrase you wish to insert. He does not see you as the helpful, beneficial person he thinks he met a few hours or days ago. He sees you as the stereotypical thief we, salespeople, are all supposed to be. As much as it hurts (and I know it hurts), you have to give him his money back. Your willingness to do right by him may cause him to think doing business with you may be in his best interest after all. Perhaps he will rethink his stance and allow you to "resell" him. Perhaps he will not. At the very least, it will show him that, not only do you have his best interests at heart, but you are only eager to help those who are willing to help themselves.

When you satisfy the needs of your customers, they will multiply themselves through friendly referrals. If, on the other hand, you under-deliver on your promises, in effect stealing their money, you will either become the subject of a nasty hate blog or suffer a very public professional "death by Twitter". Today, if people hate you, they can tell billions of people just by pressing a button. In the end, the choices you make in dealing with unsatisfied customers boil down to what you would rather lose: one little commission or your entire professional reputation. As promised, I've done the best I can to guide you. The ball, as they say (whomever "they" are), is in your hands. Run hard with it. Score over and over with it. Most of all, though, don't drop it!

VI.   When the Sell?!

Now!

The Beginning